IN THE FACE OF FEAR

In the Face of Fear

Harvey Thomas

with

Judith Gunn

Marshalls

Marshalls Paperbacks
Marshall Morgan & Scott
3 Beggarwood Lane, Basingstoke, Hants, RG23 7LP, UK

First published by Marshall Morgan & Scott Ltd,
a division of Marshall Pickering.

British Library CIP data

Thomas, Harvey
  In the face of fear.
  1. Thomas, Harvey 2. Conservative Party—
Biography 3. Public relations consultants—
Great Britain—Biography 4. Brighton (East
Sussex)—History—Bombing, 1984
  I. Title II. Gunn, Judith
  658.4'562'0924   JN1129.C72

  ISBN 0–551–01287–0

Photograph of 25th Anniversary (October 20th, 1984) of
Margaret Thatcher's election as MP for Finchley, reproduced
by kind permission of Graham Grieves, Finchley, London.

Photograph of Harvey & Marlies Thomas, reproduced by kind
permission of Universal Pictorial Press & Agency Ltd., London.

Photographs of the Grand Hotel, Brighton, reproduced by kind
permission of the Evening Argus, Brighton.

Phototypeset by Input Typesetting Ltd.
Printed in Great Britain by Anchor Brendon Ltd, Tiptree, Essex.

Contents

Foreword

It isn't everyone who is blown skyward via an exploded bomb, then lands in a pile of rubble unhurt. But knowing Harvey Thomas as well as I do, I am not surprised that it happened to him. Harvey is an exceptional person in many respects, possessing several natural talents as well as Holy Spirit-bestowed gifts.

We first met in Honolulu, Hawaii more than twenty years ago, in the radio studios of KAIM, the headquarters of The Christian Broadcasting Association, one of the ministries of The Billy Graham Evangelistic Association, where we both served in radio ministry. Although he was quite a young Christian, I was deeply impressed with his spiritual maturity, his Bible knowledge and well-balanced, practical application of scripture truth. I recall him as an enthusiastic advocate of 'faith that works'.

In this book, one may expect some fascinating reading – a happy combination of his Christian testimony as a conservative evangelical, and his deep-seated conviction that it is honouring to God when born-again Christian believers take an active part in the professions and civil affairs. 'Both of these (says the author) are sadly needed today.' I agree.

My prayer is that our God, who loves all people everywhere, may use this writing of my very dear friend, to His glory.

Wendell P. Loveless
Honolulu, Hawaii
August 1985

1: Brighton '84

There was one day of Conference left and so far, it had gone well. That afternoon Norman Tebbit had given a rousing speech which had brought the representatives to their feet for an extended standing ovation. Conference itself was running smoothly and now, on the last night, the parties were in full swing.

It was October 11th, 1984 and Marlies, my wife, was already five days overdue on the date given her for the birth of our first child. I was the Conference's Technical Co-ordinator, used to administration and planning ahead and yet, as with many of the best laid plans, the arrival of our baby seemed as though it would coincide with the biggest event in the Conservative Party's annual calendar! Just before I left for Brighton that week I had half-jokingly said to Marlies 'Please, whatever you do, don't have it on the 12th of October'. That was the last day of the Conference, traditionally the day on which the Prime Minister gives her key-note speech and I needed to concentrate totally on the presentation of it.

So I had come to Conference prepared for a dash back to London should the need arise. I was wearing a 'bleeper' which meant I could be reached anywhere in the UK. Marlies had only to dial the number that activated the bleep and I could be with her inside an hour and a half. Every night I went to bed making sure that the bleeper was switched on.

That Thursday had been a long day and I was expecting to do some staff work for the next day but it was now eleven p.m. and I was still not needed; so I decided to go to bed to snatch what sleep I could. I knew that I might get a 'phone call in the small hours of the morning so I returned to my seventh floor room, fully expecting an interrupted night – I did not even begin to suspect how dramatic that interruption would be.

I was in Brighton staying in the Grand Hotel because for six years I had been Public Relations and Special Projects Consultant with the Conservative Party. Specifically, this meant that I dealt with a great deal of the visual and conference presentation, the setting up of election rallies and television training.

My involvement with the organisation of big rallies and conferences goes back to 1961 when I began to work with the Billy Graham Association at the Maine Road Stadium in Manchester. That was the start of a long, fascinating period of my life as a part of the Team on the various crusades and congresses that the Billy Graham Association pioneered.

During that time I visited no less than ninety-seven countries. I was mostly out of the United Kingdom for eighteen years and I met a great many men and women both of God and of modern history. It is hardly surprising that my interest in Public Relations grew while I was involved in this work. I can remember one specific event that illustrated graphically to me the power of PR.

I was flying from Darwin to Brisbane, in the late sixties – a journey of about two thousand miles across the outback and Australia's Northern Territory with one stop at Mt. Isa, a small mining town in Queensland. Because of the nature of my work, I had already done a great deal of flying and so to make my journeys easier

10

I had VIP status with the Airline. I also knew enough to know when something was wrong, and that day we were flying too low. I hazarded a guess as to what was up and asked the air hostess, 'What's happened to your third engine?' She replied doubtfully that I wasn't supposed to know – which I didn't find very encouraging.

Our difficulties meant that the landing at Mt. Isa airport merited emergency status, that meant one rickety fire engine belting down the runway far behind us – thankfully we didn't need it. We were all asked to disembark and I, with my VIP status, was shown into an air-conditioned lounge while the other passengers had to sit it out in the searing Mt. Isa heat of over one hundred degrees fahrenheit.

I had not been waiting long, when an aboriginal gentleman in white mechanic's overalls came into the room and opened the window – not the thing to do in an air-conditioned room. Then he picked up the 'phone and began talking to Brisbane. After a moment he told them to hold on and he went to the window and yelled to a colleague who was positioned up the back end of this Boeing's engine. 'Can you see a nut marked "A"?'

'Yes' came the distant reply. Then he went back to the 'phone and listened for a moment and yelled back 'Turn it three times to the left'. This was how that plane was fixed – on telephone instructions from Brisbane!

By this time I was feeling slightly apprehensive, but as I boarded the plane I told myself that the pilot wouldn't take off unless he was satisfied that it was safe. We found ourselves flying alongside one of those huge electrical storms that you see in Northern Australia. The clouds were just churning in the sky like great black cotton balls and jagged flashes of lightning leapt from cloud to cloud. It was a fantastic panorama.

But then the captain's voice came over on the plane's

11

intercom. 'Good afternoon ladies and gentlemen, I'm sure you're all admiring that storm over to our left. It's quite a show, but I think I ought to tell you that Brisbane's on the other side of it!' He paused to let that sink in and then went on. 'I want you all to imagine, a cork in a bucket of water. You can do anything to that cork, push it under, flick it up, put it on its side, make it somersault – but it will always float back to the surface unharmed.' He paused again. 'Now ladies and gentlemen that's what this plane is like: this plane will do anything in that storm, we may even turnover or do a somersault, but it will not do the plane any harm. I've got two computers up here'.

I heard a voice say 'What about us?', and the captain went on 'Oh yes and two other pilots, so we'll be through the storm in about five minutes. What I want you to do, is strap yourselves in, hang on tight, and we'll just go on through.' We all strapped ourselves in and then the captain's voice asked 'Right are you ready?' There was no reply, so he repeated 'I can't hear you, are you ready?'

'Yes,' came the reluctant but audible reply and he took the plane up into a huge sweeping arc and with deliberate drama turned into the storm.

He was right! We went up and down, side to side, we flipped over so much that the luggage in the overhead racks (this was in the days before enclosed racks) slid across the ceiling of the plane and finished up on the otherside. But we came through and nobody was ill and nobody panicked.

It was on that day that I realised the power of Public Relations. The pilot had presented his case so well that everyone understood exactly what was happening and had stayed calm. That may not have been the case, had he said nothing or had he failed to communicate clearly. It seemed to me then as it does now, that at the heart of every failure in the church and in politics is a failure in communications. It was then that I decided to become permanently involved in Public Relations wherever and whenever the opportunity arose.

2: Early Days

Harvey Thomas was born in April 1939, the son of a barrister and the eldest of two boys. His parentage is Welsh but he was born in Hendon and educated at Westminster School. His decision to go into Public Relations, taken on that plane over the Northern Territory of Australia, was not arrived at easily or quickly.

He had always been interested in communications, the medium and the message, ever since as a teenager, he had heard Billy Graham preach at Harringay Stadium in 1954. But the choices on leaving school were not wide and his father was keen that his son enter his own legal profession and become a solicitor. Harvey agreed to try it and he was articled to a firm of solicitors in London but spent only three years with them.

In his early twenties he was an athlete. He had played soccer for Westminster School where soccer first took its modern form so, not surprisingly, Harvey never played Rugby.

'I was at school with Anthony Steen, who is now the MP for South Hams. He's been an MP for many years now but when we were at school he and I played table tennis every morning for five years.

I was a runner, I got my half-mile just to a fraction of a second under two minutes and I got the mile down to about four minutes sixteen seconds, then along came Roger Bannister, and he changed athletics forever.'

His early training and interests made Harvey realise that he was not really suited to an academic office life-style. The desk work of a solicitor did not appeal to him.

Harvey was eager to be an actor or perhaps a barrister but training for the bar was a costly occupation and therefore not a practical choice.

'It was at Westminster that I first got my interest in acting. I was at school with Corin Redgrave, I remember that he played Romeo, I forget which boy played Juliet but I was either Montague or Capulet, I can't remember which but I had a few lines.' Looking back at those times, Harvey says, 'It's easier to see now what an enormous debt Gareth and I owe to our parents (Kenneth and Olga Thomas). They made huge sacrifices for years to put us through Public Schools and they were prepared to go on helping if I went to RADA.'

So Harvey auditioned for the Royal Academy of Dramatic Art (RADA), was accepted but never took up his place. His brother, Gareth Thomas, later followed in his footsteps, did train at RADA and became a successful actor. Gareth is best known recently, for his role as Blake, in 'Blake's 7' and Morgan in 'Morgan's Boy', both BBC series. Although the two boys did not attend the same school or college, they did spend time at home when they were looked after by an Austrian au pair Stephanie Lengauer whose excitable temperament was the butt of many of their jokes, but whose love made her a member of the family. 'Stephanie went on to become a successful business woman in music publishing and she is still part of our family.'

When his offer from RADA arrived, Harvey was already involved with the Billy Graham Association and it was that organisation that was to become his professional life for the next fifteen years.

Harvey had been a member and then leader of his church's youth fellowship since his conversion and in

15

the course of this involvement he had met Maurice Rowlandson, Billy Graham's representative in England. Harvey had realised that he did not want a career as a solicitor and had said as much to Rowlandson. Rowlandson suggested that he go to a Bible College in America, to Northwestern Bible College in Minneapolis. A course which he could well recommend, for Rowlandson himself had gone to Northwestern College at the instigation of Billy Graham who was then its President. Rowlandson told Harvey that the Billy Graham Team (in the shape of a man called Walter Smyth) were looking for someone to organise the land-line sound relays out of the Manchester Maine Road Stadium. This was a massive job, it involved the Crusade being connected to four hundred centres, each of them with a minimum of three churches at the other end; the modern equivalent is satellite or cable broadcasting used by Billy Graham in June 1985 in Sheffield.

So, in 1961 opportunities across the Atlantic were already attracting Harvey. It was no new hankering, he had always wanted to go to America. At school he had studied maps of New York and by the time he was thirteen he knew the Manhattan street plan by heart, he could have walked the streets of New York without the aid of such a map. America, it seemed to him, was not only an attractive proposition but a practical one. It was possible for a young man who feared reaching a dead end in England, to widen his training and experience by going to the USA. In England at the time there were no student grants, his father could not afford to pay to put him through university and he could not work enough hours to pay for himself – in America he could work his own way.

At the end of the Crusade at Maine Road Stadium in Manchester in August 1961 Harvey felt sure that God was leading him to America. He went to George Wilson, the Financial Director of the Billy Graham Association and asked for a job in America so that he could go to Northwestern Bible College. Wilson replied 'Well, if you don't mind hauling mailbags, yes come and work for us.'

'Of course', says Harvey, 'I was then an upper-middle-class Westminster School boy, so heaving mailbags in Minneapolis was about the worst thing that could happen in family eyes.' Even so his mother lent him one hundred and fifty sacrificial pounds and he took the boat to New York. There, he boarded a train for Minnesota.

'That train ride was a stunning introduction to America, he recalls. 'It was like the old trains you see in Westerns (with a platform at the back) that the old film heroes used to wave from. We stood on that platform and travelled for hundreds of miles along the banks of the Mississippi in a late summer evening. It was beautiful, I shall never forget it.

'I had one overnight stop in Chicago and I found myself walking down South State Street and quite by accident I came across the Pacific Garden Mission, a mission for down and outs. I didn't know what it was at first, but I was invited in and there I gave my Christian testimony' – the first of many such opportunities that were to open to him in America.

Harvey's testimony was a description of his faith and Christian experience. He had by then been a committed Christian for some years. His conversion took place at a Crusaders' camp on the Isle of Wight one summer when he was eleven. Like most boys of that age he was not always gripped by Christian teaching. Sitting in a dark room, studying the Bible seemed a hard thing to do on a summer's day and he let his attention wander from the Bible Class. The teacher was Dr Francis Conningsby, a magistrate in Guernsey, and an academic.

'I sat at the back of the room, and I could look out to where, in the distance, the Queen Mary (which is now permanently moored in California) was sailing off to the States. I was absorbed by this distant sight when Dr Conningsby suddenly said "Harvey!" and, of course, at that age, there is nothing more embarrassing than having your name called out in the middle of fifty boys all sitting there looking at you. I turned back sheepishly and Dr Conningsby continued "You know, if you turn your eyes on Jesus" and then he spoke the words of the well-known chorus, "and look full in His wonderful face, then the things of the earth (including the Queen Mary, Harvey) will grow strangely dim, in the light of His glory and grace." Then he stopped the class and we sung the chorus and that night I gave my life to Christ.'

It was armed with that faith, fifteen dollars and a letter from Maurice Rowlandson that Harvey arrived in Minnesota. His intention was to enrol at the North-western Bible College and he had to borrow the fifty dollars for the enrolment fee to do it, from George Wilson, of the Billy Graham Association, who for years since, has pretended it was a momentary lapse from his rigid controls of finances!

He quickly began to adapt to the American way of life, but he was a foreign student and as a result he was told that soon a second opportunity would arise for him to give his Christian testimony.

It was the tradition in the college that each foreign student was invited to preach at the morning chapel service, which was broadcast live on radio. Harvey waited in anticipation for his invitation, but time went by and he settled into the routine but with no broadcast chapel message behind him.

The college's reticence was unusual, but Harvey had a tough act to follow. Two years previously an enthusiastic Scottish student, Billy Strachan (now Principal of

Capernwray Bible School), had come to Northwestern Bible College. He had been a comedian before being converted and deciding on full-time Christian work, so his message for the American college was lively.

To enter Northwestern Bible College each student had to sign a declaration of faith. They had to assure their tutors and the college that they had been converted. No student entering the college should, in theory, have been in need of salvation. At least this was *thought* to be the case until Billy Strachan preached. He gave a sermon of such enthusiasm and evangelical fervour, that in answer to his invitation at the end of the service, several of the students went forward to give their lives to Christ all broadcast live on KTIS Radio.

Embarrassed, the college was more than wary of future foreign students, for fear that such a thing might happen again. Harvey duly gave a morning chapel message and has since kept close ties with KTIS Radio and particularly his friend Paul Ramseyer who now directs the Network Programme.

Harvey not only had to study, but work and although the rigours of a night shift were new to him he had proved his worth at Maine Road Stadium. He had been found late one night, in the small hours in fact, surrounded by paper and string dutifully wrapping parcels. His more experienced colleague Walter Smyth, took one look at the chaos and said 'That is *not* the way you wrap parcels!' and proceeded to teach Harvey a skill in wrapping parcels that has saved him time and sellotape since. This experience and stamina was now to stand him in good stead, although it was a contrast to his experience as a public schoolboy.

'I was, in colloquial British terms, the usual middle-class character. My school had been Westminster and I wore a semi-stiff collar which I put on with studs. I was very much the "frightfully nice", "terribly good chap".

19

'I went first to Westminster Underschool and then for four-and-a-half years I was at the Senior School. Westminster School is what is termed a Royal School and it enjoyed certain privileges as such. I remember when I was still at the Underschool, I was presented to King George VI. He came to open the College Garden for us – it had been closed since the War. I remember that we all stood in line and shook hands with him when he came round. It was not long before he died.'

'A few days after her coronation I was also presented to Queen Elizabeth II as a First Class Scout from Westminster School. I was a scout instead of an Army Cadet, there didn't seem to me to be much point in being an Army Cadet then. I think that now perhaps, in today's Britain, National Service and a bit of imposed discipline would not do us any harm. I can see that there could be great benefits in it. Ever since Roy Jenkins condoned the permissive age, by coining the phrase "Let it all hang out" the results in today's world were inevitable – a decline in moral and spiritual values. Those of us who were brought up in a more disciplined age find the new social environment rather nasty. In those days the discipline was to a large extent self-imposed. We didn't dream of doing some of the things that are done today, like disrupting a football match. Self restraint needs to be re-taught.

'Among the Royal privileges accorded to the pupils of Westminster School were seats in the Abbey at the coronation. I missed being in the Abbey itself for the coronation by one year. Another rather more unusual privilege was connected with the National Anthem. Westminster School pupils are the only people allowed to continue cheering while the National Anthem is played during the State Procession for the opening of Parliament. Everyone else must remain silent and stand stiffly to attention, but not the boys of Westminster School, we

20

could cheer right the way through and of course we did, with great gusto. In fact we tended to be silent as mice until the anthem was played and then we'd cheer our heads off. We used to have a certain pride in ourselves, which doesn't seem to be there so much now. We did have to wear that semi-stiff collar, which on reflection wasn't such a bad thing. The great thing about knowing how to do something, is that if you choose to reject it, at least you know what you're rejecting and you can use it again if you need it. Nowadays it seems that we take pride in being scruffy.

'It never crossed my mind at the time, but again, looking back I can see that there were a few homosexual boys at Westminster. Since my school days there have occasionally been items in the press in that connection, about one or two of my contemporaries. I don't think that the system actually made or created homosexuality in the boys – the thought certainly never occurred to me. That's a bit like blaming the environment for sinful man. I certainly didn't recognise it then. It's only that the evidence that has emerged since has made me realise it.'

His early years at the Westminster School immersed him in the traditions and attitudes of English institutions but Harvey does not consider that the School encouraged too much 'superiority' in the attitudes of its boys. Perhaps with the usual sense of loyalty that public schoolboys are expected to have for their own school, he smilingly accuses Eton of teaching people to be "stuck up". By contrast, living and working in America chased away any vestiges of incipient snobbery or class consciousness that may have been instilled in Harvey in his early years at Westminster. America was an education in new attitudes and approaches.

'Then I was in the US, working for the night mail shift, wearing overalls and this was completely foreign

21

to me. I loved it, because it was new, I found myself doing physical work as well as using my head. I realised for the first time, that somebody with a middle-class background could actually do a job with his hands. This has been a gold mine to me since because both in principle and in practice, I have been able to earn reasonable fees and salaries because I am able and willing to turn my hands to most things. I'm very grateful that there were no student grants in my day — it taught me how to work!

'I learned too about "Direct Mail". In those days the Billy Graham Association had a mailing list of around seven million. It was one of the first mailing lists to go on computer. Time Magazine, Reader's Digest and a few others were developing it at about the same time, but the technique has been used by a great many organisations since. American Express is one example, Jerry Falwell and the "New Right" are another. They have developed the system in America considerably and it originated from the Direct Mailing principles that I worked with on those night shifts.

'While I was on those shifts I learned to drive trucks to deliver the mail. Sometimes I drove them on ice. I can remember sliding along the road and I nearly drove one of those things with five tons of mail into the Mississippi one night. I was trying to back it up to the Minneapolis post office which is high above the river, and I hit this wall, I felt the wheels make contact with the ledge. I was terrified that it was going to tumble backwards down into the Mississippi taking me with it.

'Working the night shift and living in America began to teach me something that you never really learn in England and that is that there is actually no such thing as "class". You are what you are and if you have character and the ability to develop that character, then it doesn't actually matter whether you're in a traditional socio-economic group or otherwise. You are an individual not a class.'

Harvey spent two years in Minneapolis. He joined the debating teams with Northwestern Bible College and this took him to Westpoint, America's most famous military academy. They ran a debating competition in which Harvey participated.

'At school I had got five O levels. At Northwestern Bible College I increased my qualifications to go to the University of Minnesota and there I kept things at a fairly steady level of B minus C plus. I don't think that I really appreciated the value of learning. It was not until after I left the Billy Graham Team and came to work for the Conservatives that I realised how valuable training and experience is. It was only then that I began to realise that I had knowledge and had gained unique experiences.'

After he left the University of Minnesota his training became a matter of learning while he worked, his formal education was now complete, but the question was, where was he to continue his training?

'I wanted to get back into crusades, I'd been at college for two years, so I asked Walter Smyth whether this would be possible. He replied that he would think about it and then the Press Officer of the Billy Graham Organisation, Lance Zabitz contacted me. Lance had been a "Crime and Religion" reporter on the "Buffalo Evening News" in New York (in those days crime and religion seemed to go together on American local newspapers). He had a good idea of how to deal with the Press and the media. He asked Walter if I could assist him on the Los Angeles crusade.'

The L.A. crusade was held in the Olympic Stadium, recently used for the 1984 Olympic Games, but in 1963 Billy Graham drew the biggest crowd ever seen in the stadium, before or since, 134,254, many more than the ninety thousand who came to the Olympic events.

In order that the press could get a good picture of Billy Graham, Lance Zabitz arranged that they should be placed on a moveable platform in front of Billy. They could stay there and get pictures until a couple of minutes after the preaching had begun. Then, so that no one was distracted, they were asked to move and the platform, a kind of scaffolding on wheels, was moved out of the way. This was Harvey's job, but for the first couple of days he could not do it unobtrusively, because the scaffolding creaked loudly and Harvey was very conscious of it.

What Harvey learnt, he learnt unofficially from people like Bill Brown and Walter Smyth, to whom he feels he owes his early training but it was not institutional, it was really a matter of individual and voluntary tuition.

When he left college there was no real opening for him in the Billy Graham Organisation, but a chance came up to audition for KAIM radio in Hawaii, the Billy Graham Organisation's own radio station. He passed and flew to Hawaii to begin working for KAIM, AM and FM.

3: Songs and Sunshine

'I lived virtually on the beach in Hawaii. I swam a lot, and in those years I watched the sunrise each day because I had to be at KAIM by five-thirty in the morning.

'I worked on a programme called "Songs and Sunshine". It was live broadcasting which started each morning at six o'clock. I would open the show with "Good morning everybody it's six o'clock and this is Harvey Thomas welcoming you to KAIM, AM and FM in the Hawaiian Islands and in the studio with me, as always, is Wendell P. Loveless..." and I handed straight over to Wendell P.

'Wendell P. Loveless is a great character. He was in his seventies then. He is a well-known gospel songwriter. He wrote songs such as "Every day with Jesus" and "All because of Calvary". He had literally hundreds of recordings of songs that he had written, and "Songs and Sunshine" was his programme.

'It was a pot pourri of radio programming that was marvellous. We had news, comment and music, which Wendell P. chose himself, anything from classical to hot gospel. There were poems, humorous moments, sometimes interviews, with a Biblical orientation all the way through. Then Wendell would have "counselling corner" and take someone's problem and muse on it for a while. He wouldn't lecture, like today's Agony Aunts do. I find that today's public counsellors are very abrupt. They don't have a message. Without Christianity as their base they have no hope to offer but Wendell P. would quietly get the message across.

'The programme was very popular and it made a minor celebrity of myself and Wendell P. was even more well known. Whenever he or I went to the outer islands to preach, Wendell would say "Harvey's going to such and such an island tonight to preach" and he'd call out "What time are you leaving Harvey?" and I'd tell him "Aloha Airlines flight number . . . at six p.m." and as a result thirty or forty people would turn out to see me off and wish me well, just for an overnight island hop. Of course, for Wendell the crowds reached over a hundred.'

The impact of the programme was such that even today Harvey is remembered in Hawaii for his catch phrases with Wendell Loveless on "Songs and Sunshine".

Harvey's voice is still heard in Hawaii. Once a week he sends a broadcast letter to KAIM called "View From Europe". It was while working in Hawaii that Harvey began to pick up experience as a broadcaster in his own right and some of the more prestigious news assignments came his way.

Martin Luther King was one such interview. He came to Hawaii for a short visit, after the famous march to Washington and he gave Harvey Hawaii's first live interview with him.

'I spent only one half day with Martin Luther King, I travelled around with him in Hawaii. I'd always felt that Martin Luther King was a Billy Graham without the discipline. Billy Graham is a very disciplined man who recognises potential temptations and avoids them. Martin Luther King was a Baptist and had the potential to be a black Billy Graham but he had the calling to be involved in the political field. There was a degree of showmanship about him, which is no bad thing when you're trying to present a case. I had just the slightest feeling of lack of sincerity, perhaps it was a lack of implementation in his own life. Billy Graham had total personal commitment and full personal implementation of his faith in his life. He always practised what he preached.

'I was with Martin Luther King for a very short time, but it was an intense time and I listened hard. I felt that he was not the strong and disciplined man he could be. Had he been so, he might have been less open to criticism.'

Harvey had no political involvement in those days. After three years out of England, he was beginning to lose touch, he had picked up an American accent and was hardly recognisable as the public schoolboy he had once been. But KAIM brought him another interview, an interview with the then Deputy Prime Minister of England and a leader of the party that Harvey was later to work for, R. A. B. Butler.

'R. A. B. Butler came out to Honolulu and stayed at the Royal Hawaiian Hotel, which is all pink and set on Waikiki Beach. I remember there was a big fuss being made by the Americans (who haven't changed very much) because the British were trading Leyland buses with Cuba. Castro had just come to power then and the Americans said that the British were supporting a communist régime in Central America, "the soft under-belly of the USA".

'I remember asking Mr Butler in my strong American accent "Tell me sir, how do you justify trading buses with Cuba?" and he replied:

"Well you've got to remember old boy," (those were the days when British politicians still said "old boy" to anyone they considered as a colonial and he gave me the impression that he thought that was exactly what I was) "purely business, nothing political, don't approve of the fellow at all but business is business." It was the first time that I had ever met a politician and I can't say that as a top Conservative, he impressed me at that time.'

Although R. A. B. Butler had failed to impress the young Harvey Thomas, he had given Harvey a certain insight into the way politicians and particularly Conservative politicians, present themselves to the public. It made him realise, when he came to work with them, just how they looked and sounded to the ordinary man.

'Even though we're not pompous, our communications can come out as pompous! I knew I believed in the philosophy but I was nearly turned off by R. A. B. Butler's approach and that's one of my prime burdens today: to make it clear that we do care and that individuals do matter.'

One abiding memory for Harvey, that he associates with Hawaii and KAIM Radio, is one he shares with the many others who can remember the events in November 1963, when Dallas, Texas became infamous.

'It was early morning in Hawaii, because of the time difference between us and Dallas. I was on the air as usual. We'd finished "Songs and Sunshine" and there was a fifteen minute recorded programme called "The Voice of China and Asia" which we ran at eight forty-five a.m. and which gave me time to rest and eat my scrambled egg sandwiches in the kitchen. At nine o'clock we would split the two frequencies and broadcast "Master Works of Music" on FM and "The Morning Chapel Hour" on AM.

'I was sitting in the kitchen, eating my sandwiches when Doris Yonishiga, who handled KAIM's radio log, receiving the wire coming from the U.P.I. news service, dashed in and said "Harvey! Harvey! Kennedy's been

28

shot!" and I can remember getting up from the table in a rather indelicate way, as I heaved my near eighteen stone up and dropping my scrambled egg sandwich in the process. I ran through to look at the United Press wire, at the same time thinking "What can I do? Do I interrupt 'The Voice of China and Asia'?" I reached the wire room and got the small strip of paper that was printed out of the machine and it said. "Flash! Kennedy shot in Dallas." I decided to act and I interrupted the fifteen minute programme to announce the news and then a few minutes later we put both AM and FM channels together and I announced "Ladies and gentlemen the President is dead". It was a very melo-dramatic broadcast but it fitted at the time. Then we kept AM and FM combined and continued to broadcast the story, (the British Consulate in Honolulu was list-ening in, getting their news from us).

'There was something else I remember about that first wire. After announcing that Kennedy had been shot it went on to say. "Police ran up the grassy knoll (by the side of the place where the President was shot) from where the shots came"; and I am convinced to this day that that is where the shots came from. Lee Harvey Oswald might have loosed off a few shots from where he was but I have stood ten or fifteen times on the spot where Kennedy was shot and in the first place there's a huge tree (that *was* there in 1963) in Oswald's firing line. There's no way that he could have got off three shots that hit Kennedy.

'That first newsflash said that the police *ran up the grassy knoll, towards where the shots came from*. There's a parking lot there, an easy place to fire from and get away from. The police were met there by men who flashed secret service badges at them, so they turned back; but we have since learned that there were no secret service men at that spot that day. Every time I go to

29

Dallas I go and spend an hour at that place trying to work out what happened.'

Kennedy's assassination was neither the first nor the last of such events, and some twenty-one years later, Harvey was to come much closer to such an attempt.

4: Fear and Faith

'I never heard the bomb. I was about twelve feet away from it lying right on top of it, it was immediately beneath me in Room 629. I never heard the bang go off, the first thing I knew was that everything was going round and round and I was going up. I felt myself going up and fortunately the ceiling went up ahead of me, so by the time I got to where it was, it had already gone up higher and I didn't hit it. But then it (including me) all started coming down and when I got to where my room was, it wasn't there any more.

'I didn't quite know what was happening. At first I thought "Maybe it's an earthquake." Then I thought, "No, not in Brighton. Certainly not during a Tory Party Conference!" By this time everything was hitting me. Bits of timber, masonry and beams were bouncing off me and I was twisting in the air so much so that when I landed, a sheet had wrapped itself round my neck.

'By now I had woken up – really woken up – and I was very alert. I am thankful now that I had not gone to the parties and that I am teetotal and a non-smoker, for I'm sure that in those first few seconds I was more alert, because of it. Instinctively I put my hands up to my face and covered my nose and mouth.

'It is extraordinary how things come back to you in moments of crisis and how you don't react the way you think you're going to. You'd expect to panic! If anyone had told me that I would be blown up and buried in a bomb explosion, I would have assumed that in such a situation I'd panic, but I didn't. I was actually too busy! There wasn't any time and already a passage of the New Testament had come back to me: 1 John 1 verse nine "If you confess your sins, He is faithful and just to forgive you your sins." I had realised by then that my death was not going to be immediate. As a preacher I had often warned people that their deaths could come at any moment, quickly and without warning, no time to repent. Probably, more often than not, it's not like that. I certainly had time to prepare myself for eternity and I heard myself say out loud. "Lord, if I have got anything left unconfessed, then please take it as read!" Of course I hadn't got time to go into detail but I was grateful for those few seconds, for as I fell down those three floors (having gone up one) I was absolutely convinced that I was going to die.'

It was Harvey's faith that was to sustain him through the next few hours, as well as his physical bulk and fitness and perhaps, most of all, the miracle that had saved him from major injury or pain. But it was not the first time that Harvey had been in fear for his life. Previous expeditions on behalf of the Billy Graham Organisation had occasionally left him wondering as to his safety but such events were to provide him with the faith that now helped him through his fear.

In 1969 Harvey was in Australia. Now a full-time employee of the Billy Graham Organisation, he was working on setting up crusades and stimulating interest in the work for the Billy Graham Team. This meant a great deal of travelling and therefore flying.

'I'd never really relaxed flying. I wasn't exactly scared, I wasn't frightened as such but I never ate on the plane (and I was flying all over the world by then) and I was never relaxed, my stomach was the tiniest bit

32

questioning. The moment I thought "Well I'll just have a cup of coffee" we invariably hit turbulence, wherever we were.

'On this occasion I was flying into the depths of Papua New Guinea. I had flown from Sydney to Port Moresby and then from there, over the mountains in a Fokker Friendship, a two engined propeller-driven plane, which, in itself, was a bit dicey. We landed again and my hosts the Wycliffe Bible Translators had one of their missionaries pick me up from this airstrip in a single engine Cessna – and then we did some real flying! At one point we got so close to the top of the mountains that the thirteen foot tall elephant grass that grows on the side of those mountains actually hit our undercarriage and attached itself to our wheels.

'But that wasn't all, as we came in to land we seemed to be flying straight into the side of the mountain. I watched apprehensively as the cliff loomed nearer, then suddenly, just before we hit, we veered upwards, up the side of the mountain until a small ledge appeared just beneath us and then quickly we levelled parallel with the ledge and dropped onto it. This ledge was the landing strip. At one end was the sheer drop we had just come up from, at the other was more mountain and we had to stop pretty sharpish in order not to hit the mountain at the other end.

'The problem was that the ledge was too short to take an ordinary landing approach. If you tried it, you would not have time to brake and you would just crash into the mountain so we had to approach it from below, fly up to it, slowing up sufficiently to just 'plop' over the edge and stop in time. Taking off was slightly easier of course, you just flew off the edge!

'Anyway once we were safely landed, we walked for about three hours through some very dense jungle, with a fair amount of wildlife in evidence. We had to stop at one point to let a huge python, about six inches in width and thirty feet long, cross the path in front of us.

'My experiences with reptiles have not always been as uneventful as that encounter. I remember once in Darwin, which is a few hundred miles south of New Guinea, I was taken to a crocodile farm.'

In the Northern Territory there are two breeds of crocodile, Johnson's or the fresh water crocodile which looks rather like an alligator and the salt water crocodile. While the fresh water crocodile is not known to have attacked man, the salt water crocodile, living in the estuaries, is notorious for its ferocity, Harvey, however, was not fully aware of this fact.

'This salt water crocodile had been caught the night before and taken into the crocodile farm. It was thirteen to fifteen feet long. To me it really was a big crocodile so I went to have a look at it. I had a broomstick and I promise I wasn't prodding it! I just sat and watched it.

'There was a three foot high wall surrounding the area in which this crocodile was kept and my broomstick was hanging over the side slightly. I didn't realise that these things could jump but suddenly this huge animal launched itself out of the water and bit the broomstick off six inches away from my hand. I learnt the benefits of a fast reaction that day, believe me!

'But a fast reaction was not advisable in the face of the python that we observed in New Guinea, we had to wait and watch it sedately pass.

'Finally we reached the village and were met by the resident missionaries. The couple who greeted us, were a resourceful pair for they had rigged up an interesting system for getting water from their local stream into their hut. They had built a series of wooden channels and chutes that dipped into the stream. You pulled the chute at your end and down came the water into the sink, along occasionally, with a few unwelcome slithery guests. Once I was introduced, I was taken to the village and greeted by the native inhabitants. My pilot now became my interpreter and I began to speak.

'I told them that I was glad to be there; but that I had had a hard journey. I didn't like being in the sky, it was frightening and bumpy. Although I thought Doug was a very good pilot, I preferred the big plane. Then one of the audience made a comment and I asked Doug what he had said. "Oh it doesn't matter" said Doug, so I knew it did and I pressed him harder so that, at last, he relented. "Well, accurately translated," he said. "it means that if you had a little more faith, then you wouldn't mind the bumps in my plane."

'From that day on I have flown like a baby and eaten like a horse on every flight. It was a fascinating lesson in faith, I went miles to learn it and I received it from an unlikely source; from a so-called ignorant native, who had a far greater understanding of what faith was than I did.'

By now Harvey was proving to be an invaluable Billy Graham Team member. In 1966, before travelling to Australia, he had returned to England to assist Bill Brown in the setting up of the Billy Graham Crusade in Earls Court where Cliff Richard first sang out his public declaration of faith.

As the sixties drew to a close Harvey flew to Australasia to work. Because of the illness of his boss there, he found himself in charge and gained valuable experience in a hectic two years. New Guinea had brought him a new insight into the nature of faith and that flight across the outback of Australia, proved to him the value of PR and communications. It decided for him the direction that he would follow in the next few years. It had set him on the path that would lead him to Brighton in 1984.

5: Travelling with the Team

'I was still in Australia in sixty-nine when I got a 'phone call from Walter Smyth in Europe. After we'd said "Hello" he said:

"Harvey, I'd like to see you on Friday."

"Fine" I said, "when are you coming over?"

"I'm not, you're coming to Copenhagen."

"Oh great, how long for?"

"I don't know, just get packed and come."

'So I went to Copenhagen and there Walter said to me "We're going to have a Crusade in Europe."

"Great" I said. "Where?"

"Europe"

"Europe's a big place!"

"Well that's up to you Harvey. We're going to have a crusade based in Dortmund in north Germany and we'd like to do it by closed circuit TV in as many cities in Europe as would want to have Billy there in the flesh"

'So I spent the next three months going round Europe, knocking on doors and asking "Would you like to have a Billy Graham Crusade on closed circuit TV in your town?" Upon which most people would reply "Pardon?" in their various languages. We finally had thirty-six closed circuit TV connections and broadcast simultaneously in seven different countries – that was Euro '70.'

Harvey was now to become involved in the hectic

36

work of setting up the crusades and rallies of Billy Graham's early seventies campaigning. A work which was to bring him into close contact with the evangelist himself.

'I can't remember the first time I met Billy Graham. People's *positions* have never impressed me, people are ordinary, whatever their posts. It's the *person* who impresses, important or otherwise.

'I've seen a photograph of myself in a group of staff at the Manchester, Maine Road Stadium crusade in 1961 and I know we all met Billy and shook hands with him then. I had heard him once at Harringay in 1954 and that was what triggered my interest in his ministry. I'd been a Christian for a few years by then and I'd sat through some pretty poor communications (then I was bored – now I think of them as being bad communications) and then suddenly I was at Harringay and there was life in the Christian message!

'One of the more unusual memories I have of Billy, but one which reminds me that the life in that message didn't come without cost, happened when I was in a car with Billy in Brussels. I was driving and everything seemed quite normal when suddenly Billy yelled "Yes! Yes! No! No!" at the top of his voice and I nearly drove down a ditch. I wondered what on earth was happening. Perhaps Billy was having a private conversation with God and was trying to make himself heard. But Grady Wilson in the back of the car just laughed and told me that this shouting was part of his voice training. Apparently the words 'yes' and 'no' between them exercise every muscle involved in speech. I must admit I was taken by surprise.'

Putting over that message in an exciting and stimulating way was not a task that came easily to the Graham Team. It was the result of prayer, months of hard work, and hard learned experience. As a PR consultant now,

37

it is Harvey's intention that all the work that goes into presenting a politician, evangelist or an event, should not be in evidence to the eyes of the public or the person involved. Everything should run smoothly and efficiently and the speaker should not be embarrassed by microphones at the wrong height or a failure of the Master of Ceremonies to guide the event efficiently.

The Crosby by-election in 1981 was a nightmare for Harvey because it was one of those occasions where the practicalities of running a meeting became all too clear to those involved.

'It was definitely an example of how *not* to run a campaign meeting. I think there had been the same Conservative MP in Crosby for years and he died, leaving no organisation for a back-up campaign. Everyone thought it was a safe Conservative seat and as a result Shirley Williams won it – temporarily.

'One particular evening at Crosby we were holding a meeting at a school. Now I had been warned that the caretaker was unsympathetic to the Conservative cause and that was his right. But he had locked up the entire school, except for the ladies' room and the men's room and the hall itself. He locked up everything and vanished. I could find nothing I needed and if I could have found it, I probably couldn't have got at it. Anyway, there was an unusually big crowd that evening. Sir Geoffrey Howe was the speaker and it was getting hot in the hall even though it wasn't that hot outside.

'The first thing I had to improvise was a Public Address system so I got two small speakers off the cars we used to campaign in the streets; the sort of loud speakers that allow you to drive round the streets talking to the public through a loud hailer and I used these to rig up a PA system. I had to stretch every wire as far as it would go but it was working and nothing was in

38

view, even though the wires were six inches above the ground at the *back* of the platform.

'There was not only a big crowd but they had started coming in early so I put some cassette taped music through this PA system. I had a tape of some marching band music so I put that on and went off to look for a jug of water. Of course everything was locked up including the kitchen and the only tap I could find didn't look very hygienic. Frustrated, I returned to the hall only to find that the entire audience was standing stiffly on its feet for no immediately apparent reason. No speaker had arrived and nobody was on the platform. No, but the National Anthem was playing on the tape I'd put on and the whole audience had dutifully risen to its feet to honour the Queen! Once it was over, I went and checked the tape to make sure it didn't have any other anthems on it and then let it play on. Certain that it wouldn't happen again I dashed out, still looking for water because that's normally the last thing you do before a meeting. In the end I had to get two volunteers to go out to the surrounding houses and borrow a jug of water and half-a-dozen glasses.

In the meantime the platform party had arrived and sat down. At this point the Chairman of the meeting, for no apparent reason and without a word to me asked the young people to come down to the front and sit on the floor surrounding the platform. Well the wires for the PA were very vulnerable behind the platform and of course, the whole thing went 'phut'! Everything quit and Sir Geoffrey had to get up and speak to the assembled large crowd, in a hot room, with no PA and no water – at least not at first! The water arrived ten minutes later when the two volunteers returned triumphantly and interrupted Sir Geoffrey's speech to provide him with water.'

There, for Harvey, the organisation of a meeting was

far too obvious. Indeed the main speaker himself had noticed the difficulties and remarked the following year after a meeting which had gone very smoothly, as it should have done at Crosby. "It's so nice to see your things working Harvey" (he was referring to an electronic lectern) and he went on to say "I shall *never* forget Crosby!"

The ideal is that a meeting or a rally should be arranged and the participants would never know how much work has gone into it. All they should know is that everything functions smoothly.

But although by 1981 at the Crosby by-election Harvey had become fully ensconsed in the political world, in the early seventies politics were only gradually beginning to impinge on his awareness.

Working with Billy Graham through the early seventies gave Harvey a chance to observe the evangelist at a time when political controversy and speculation surrounded the influential figures of American public life, including Billy Graham.

The questions and the anguish hanging over the bitter struggle in Vietnam, were commented upon by all those who shared in the conflict or watched it take its course but one man remained silent, Billy Graham. In Lausanne Harvey took advantage of a chance to ask him why.

"I know too much about it to make public declarations." replied Graham "I knew just how complicated it was. What could I say to Kissinger? You know you're going to kill one hundred thousand people and that it is wrong to kill at all, that it is murder – but on the other hand, if you know that five hundred thousand *more* people will be killed if you don't kill that first one hundred thousand people, what do you do? I'm just thankful I never had to make those decisions."

And what of Nixon? The man who made such an

impregnable mark on American history. Was Billy Graham surprised by what was eventually found out?

"Yes, you know I've known Richard Nixon for nearly twenty years and in all that time I've never heard him swear." Nixon was clearly a man who adopted a different style of language to suit those with whom he spoke – a chameleon.

The controversy surrounding Billy Graham at the time was not disturbing. As Harvey points out, Billy Graham had nothing to be afraid of, there was nothing to be found out!

'I know that Billy Graham always steered clear of politics. He knew all the presidents (since Eisenhower) whatever their party. Nixon was certainly not the one he knew best. It was only that mass communication really came into its own then and Billy's association with the White House became public knowledge; but it was there long before Watergate and Vietnam, as it is now in 1985.'

The pace in the early seventies left little time for personal life or politics for Harvey. Euro '70 the closed circuit TV crusade was soon followed by an International Congress in Amsterdam and then by a big event in London – Spiritual Re-Emphasis '73, SPRE-E '73.

Spre-e '73 was a week long event at which Billy Graham preached every night and which finished with a rally at Wembley Stadium on the Saturday afternoon. Eleven thousand young people came to Earls Court to hear the evangelist preach and spend the days learning and evangelising on the streets. It was a hot week and London swarmed with people carrying Spre-e '73 carrier bags, Spre-e badges or Spre-e newspapers in the streets and the underground singing choruses, to such an extent that London Transport complained that the singing was drowning out the platform announcements.

41

For Harvey, amongst the many logistical problems in which he shared was one unexpected problem.

'There were forty-eight of us in one office, in a very hot summer and it begun to get a bit high to say the least. Those were the days before deodorants were routine. The problem became so noticeable that Maurice Rowlandson said to me "Harvey, you're American trained, why don't you give us all a lecture in personal hygiene?" So we went out and got forty-eight rolls of polo mints and forty-eight spray deodorants and the next morning Maurice got us all together and I gave a little talk to these men and women on how, where and what to wash and what to do when you've finished! Then finally I said "Right, I'll lead the way and we'll all take one of these sprays and one of these packets and off we go."

'The following morning Linda, a young woman who had attended the lecture came up to me (with a very straight face) and said. "I had a little problem this morning Harvey."

"Oh what?"

"Well I finally managed to get that spray in my mouth but I'm having terrible trouble keeping these mints under my arms!" She really had me worried, she said it with such a straight face.'

Spre-e '73 proved sufficiently successful (possibly helped by Harvey's efforts to keep everyone working together and still remaining friends) that a European event in Brussels was planned for 1975.

'There were a lot of problems in 'Eurofest', internally as well as externally. I think some of it was related to Spre-e. The Graham Team had to cover a lot of the cost of Spre-e and they worried that they would have to spend the same amount again. But this time we actually had very tight budgeting all the way through so we remained steady, except in the last three weeks.

'In Eurofest we had eight thousand people from forty-seven different countries in Brussels. We worked on a representative system, so we had representatives from all the European countries as well as the Middle East.

'The Palais du Centenaire was the campsite. We had a huge camping area, we dug lavatories and put in water mains, we had two huge halls which slept two thousand people in each: boys in one and girls in the other, row upon row of sleepers. It was not without its drama though. One morning we awoke to find that a young man had committed suicide, he had hung himself from a tree in the middle of the camp. His dissatisfaction with life was tragic, the dissatisfaction of some others we were able to find slightly more amusing.

'Some members of various contingents were not happy with the standard of cuisine that was provided. After they had all gone and we were cleaning up, we discovered tins of dog and cat food that had been bought by some of our more exotic representatives who preferred this food to that which they were offered by the camp organisers.'

Harvey prepared the electronic media that would carry voices and teachings of the speakers to the listeners, whether in a stadium or across the airwaves. Years of work with sound systems has enabled Harvey to extend the range of many a political statement or Christian sermon.

'We had forty-six thousand people in the stadium in Lausanne in 1974 and there we tried a new technique. I discovered a principle by which I now work and that is that 'sound' is like water. When you want to have a Public Address system, if you treat the sound like water you'll cover the area you want. It's like the comparisons between a shower and a hose: if you put your finger over the hose you get a more directional but less even flow.

If you put a shower head on it you cover a more general area.

'In Lausanne we had a stadium seven hundred feet high and exposed to a wind that came straight off the French Alps, across Lake Geneva and across the top of the stadium but it blew in one direction, it also blew the sound. I had to make facilities for simultaneous translation that could be heard by those who should hear German and not the French translation meant for other ears, all without earphones.

'So we hung dozens of small speakers in the German end about ten feet high so that everyone walked just beneath them and the wind blew the extra sound away from the French sections. The sound, like water, was dropped on to the heads of the German audience.

'Later in Eurofest we had the speakers in the huge Palais du Centenaire hall, directly over the heads of the people and we had eleven translations going simultaneously.

'Testing all those speakers to make sure they were all working and connected to the right microphone and speaker was a job in itself and we started at about six forty-five p.m., half an hour before the doors were due to open and an hour before Billy was due to preach. The sound technician said to me "Look Harvey, get up there and preach and the interpreters will get into their booths and translate for real and I'll check it's all working." He had a car to drive round the hall checking each section.

'He set off on his travels and I got up into the pulpit and did a take-off of Billy preaching. I used all his phrases "I want you to open your Bibles to John's gospel and chapter three". A phrase-by-phrase translation was going on in all the different languages and there we stood belting this out for twenty minutes. I preached a real sermon. I was preaching ad hoc but it was the genuine stuff while the sound man was driving frantically round in his car checking out the different sets of speakers. The time for opening the doors was fast approaching but at last he called out to me "We're nearly finished Harvey but keep going" and he continued to chase round this vast empty hall, while I preached using every gesture of Billy's. Having worked with the Team for fifteen years I knew his mannerisms well. When the checking came to an end, I said "I'm going to ask you to get up out of your seats and come forward here to the platform" and I went on "Tonight we're going to ask you to give your life to Jesus Christ and make a public confession of what you're doing." Finally the car stopped and I heard "Okay Harvey, that's it."

'And I said "And all the people said Amen!" and a hand came on my shoulder and a familiar North Carolina voice said "Harvey, I wish you'd preach that sermon for me tonight." Billy had been behind me on the platform all the time.'

Such were the hazards of testing a system thoroughly and realistically. Nevertheless the principles of testing, rehearsing and checking were now a routine part of Harvey's work in PR and communications, as was his discovery that made the translation of that sermon so much more effective. 'Sound is like water' says Harvey, but water, such a useful metaphor in the conference hall, was to prove lethally dangerous to Harvey as he lay trapped and waiting for rescue in Brighton nine years later.

6: Buried but Praying

'Even as I was going up I was thinking "breathe". If I could breathe I had hope physically. Instinctively I had raised my hands to my face. I hooked the thumb of my right hand on to my nose, so that the rest of my hand was over the left side of my face and mouth, then I put my left hand underneath my right hand facing the other way and that made an air pocket about six inches long and three inches high. "Whatever happens" I thought. "I must protect my breathing."

'And then we hit, with a tremendous crash. I had landed on a girder sticking out over a five storey drop and there I was trapped while a ten ton load of rubble came down on top of me.

'As I had thought, I now had very little air, except that which I had managed to catch in my air pocket, which gave me a degree of protection from the dust and rubble. My eyes were closed and covered in rubble and I couldn't move an inch. I remember saying aloud "Lord, I've *really* got to trust you now."

'Once I had landed, everything was still for a moment. I could hear someone calling for help and I could hear water. Then suddenly there was a tremendous crash very near to me. This was the chimney, that had been damaged by the explosion. It fell past me, missing me by about two feet and it was the chimney that caused most of the death and injury. Donald and Muriel Mclean

46

in Room 629 below in whose bathroom the bomb had been placed, and Gordon and Jean Shattock in Room 628 were directly affected by the explosion itself. The Tebbits, the Wakehams and the others were caught by the huge falling chimney that flipped the floors over as it crashed down.

'Again everything went quiet. This time all I could hear was the water and firebells. The firebells encouraged me, because hearing them meant that I wasn't buried too deep under the rubble. It would not take people days to get to me as it had some people in the explosion in Beirut. Rescue workers would be working non-stop to get us out. I knew from what I had seen before, that our rescue services would not rest until they had found everybody. Someone would be looking for us.

'The water was a different matter. I thought that it was raining and that the Grand Hotel's roof had collapsed as a result of the water. At this time, I thought that only I and a few others were affected by it and I reasoned that if all that was on top of me was a roof and ceiling, perhaps I could shift it. I was, after all eighteen and a half stone and I should be able to move a bit of timber, plaster and tiles. I tried but I couldn't move an inch, except for my left leg which I could lift about a foot. The rest of me was pinned under ten feet of rubble weighing some ten tons. It was, of course, a good thing that I couldn't move my hands because had I taken them away from my face, I would have been smothered instantly by the rubble.

'Now the water was pouring down into my mouth and nose. Although I thought it was raining, in fact the explosion had fractured the cold water tanks and mains in the hotel's roof and that was pouring down through the rubble, bringing with it dirt and particles and blocking oxygen holes. I began to choke. I couldn't breath properly anyway, because there was so much

47

pressure on my chest. In order to breathe I had to train myself to take short little breaths and I had to regulate my speed of breathing. At first, I was panting and I had to slow down to save the air. The water was proving a real threat. I couldn't swallow it, it was going down my nose as well as my mouth and it was bringing bits which were blocking my air passages.

'The only way I could control it was to put my top lip out over my lower lip. I caught the water on my right hand and guided it down onto my left hand and thus down on to the side of my face. Some water was still going into my mouth but at least most of it was channelled away over my chin and face and I could breathe. I felt that I was running out of air so I had to be careful.

'Having established, mostly involuntarily, the position I was going to be in for the next two-and-a-half hours, I had time to think and pray. I remembered the verse "If you pray, you have to pray with faith" It's amazing how your faith increases to meet the need when you're absolutely dependent on God, when you *must* depend on God, when you know you have *nothing* to offer yourself – your faith increases. By this time I had realised that I was not dead yet – and although I was completely buried, I was basically unhurt. I said "Lord, I want to see Marlies again and our baby – I don't believe that you want to take me away from them now so I'll trust you to get me out of this."

'It is very difficult to put this faith into words, because it might seem there was some special reason for *my* rescue when others did not survive. I do not presume to know why, all I can talk about is what happened to me. It was much worse for many others, for those waiting outside and for the bereaved. Marlies and I pray regularly for those who lost loved ones and particularly for Norman and Margaret Tebbit and John Wakeham who

48

suffered such pain in that rubble and who have shown such tremendous courage in dealing with it. All I had to do was lie still and wait and God gave me the strength and peace of mind to do just that.'

7: From Crusades to Conservatives

'It was when I was flying back from Australia one time in the mid-seventies that I began to wonder whether I shouldn't return to England permanently. I found that as I travelled, people were laughing at my British Passport. They were always making sarcastic remarks about it. It happened again in 1976, coming back from Argentina. I got to somewhere in West Africa, and the sarcasm was much in evidence. The gist of what they were saying was to mock the state of once proud Britain. "Look at the old country now, old England" they said "it's not the same country as it used to be!"

'I finally got a bit fed up with this but it began to make me think. I'd been out of the country almost constantly for eighteen years. I had never voted because I'd never been in the country to vote but I knew instinctively that I was a Conservative. I also knew that nowhere in the world had there been a successful socialist government at any time in history. The principle was fundamentally flawed. It seemed to me that it is impossible to give out money if you haven't earned it. How can you redistribute what isn't there?

'The United Kingdom was borrowing vast amounts of money and we were tremendously in debt to the International Monetary Fund. I couldn't see what that would solve because nobody was balancing the books. When I visited the UK in the seventies I discovered that the Labour councils of places like Sheffield and Newcastle were employing people to do things like count flowers in the park, or paint coal white or in London's Harringay, to look after the horses but there weren't any! That was ludicrous. It wasn't even political, it was just crooked!

'I believed in personal freedom; choice; looking after people who needed it but not chucking money at those who didn't; as little governmental control of the individual as possible and defending the country. I had to be a Conservative because no other philosophy made any sense.

'I decided that the only way to stop people laughing at my British Passport was (at least for my own conscience's sake) to go back and to help a bit. I felt it was unfair to criticise without doing anything about it.'

Harvey made his decision to come back to England in 1977. His years with the Billy Graham Organisation had established his faith and his career but his experience with the Team had had some hard points. The pace had been furious and with Team members travelling all over the globe the toll and strain on family life was considerable. It was an area that Harvey felt afterwards needed far more awareness and attention.

'I would frequently work eighteen to nineteen hours a day and be away from any base for months on end. I learned a lot from it but if I went back I would do a lot of things differently. In a sense it's much easier to be a Christian in a secular profession than to be a Christian working professionally amongst other Christians. There is a kind of "Christian ghetto" as Dave Foster (a colleague) called it, a whole inner society that functions within itself. If you're in it you're constantly being examined by your peers, mostly not on professional criteria

51

but personally and spiritually. Christians can be very self righteous, they're often very keen to point the finger – if only to divert attention away from themselves. Somehow I always seemed to help and encourage and pray for other people but there seemed to be *very* few people who were ready to do the same for me.

'I remember once in Bangkok we had taken a trip down the river, on a small boat and the water was filthy! There were dead animals floating in it, people urinating and dumping their rubbish in it, they were also washing in it and drinking from it. As we chugged along I noticed a woman cleaning her teeth in this revolting canal and the American with me said "You know somebody ought to tell that woman that you should brush your teeth up and down not across like that."

'Christians can be a lot like that and forget that the use of the right spiritual jargon around other Christians may hide a whole world of problems underneath. Today I think the Graham Team recognise this more.'

Harvey returned to England to offer his services to the Conservative Party.

'I met Andrew Rowe, who is now MP for mid-Kent and who was then Director of Community Affairs at Conservative Central Office. I simply said "What can I do? How can I help?" There must have been any number of people who wrote to the Conservatives and said roughly the same thing but who were politely refused. But Andrew, who had never met me before, said "Well, what do you do?" So I held up pictures of some of the big rallies I'd organised, aerial photographs of huge crowds at crusades and I said "This!"

'Andrew got one thousand pounds out of a wealthy businessman, independently of the Conservative Party's budget and gave that to me as an honorarium to try a couple of things and see how they went. I agreed to give some time between then and the next election, which we thought was going to be nearer than it finally turned out to be. Jim Callaghan chickened out in September 1978 and dropped himself into the winter of discontent. I had a very good offer from a chain of hotels in America and I intended to accept it after doing my bit for the Conservatives in the 1979 General Election.

'When I began work for them, I asked to be introduced to the person who set up and organised their Rallies and Conferences. "What do you mean 'set up'?" I was asked.

'I said "Well who coordinates the presentation? Who liaises with the media, sets up the stage, the sound, lights and all the TV presentation?"

"Oh well, there's usually someone who puts out the microphone!"

"Right!" I said. "Lead me to it!" '

Harvey had now spent nearly twenty years working with an American organisation. He had been trained in American methods and he had learnt to package and present a message. Public Relations is in many ways an American invention. They have long since been selling their Presidents to voters on television. Although Harvey was taught by the American culture and uses a great deal of what he has learned, his thoughts on the American Public Relations industry now, are not without criticism.

'American PR has deteriorated in recent years. Individual Americans can be wonderful but having worked with many, I have watched quite a change in attitude. The Americans certainly developed PR and made it a force to be reckoned with and they exported it to us. Just as it would be true to say that Europe is in a post Christian era, in the same way the Americans have brought PR to Europe with their aggressive professionalism, but now they've lost the way themselves. They have become diluted. Nowadays their PR is smooth, polished and slick. Bright young executives use the basic media techniques to make sure that the only place the public looks is at the spot they want them to focus on. The guts has gone out of American PR and it's all become a glossy package.

'I was on Hilly Rose's Radio Programme on KGMB in Hollywood on the night John Wayne died and he said to me on the air, "Harvey we've just heard that John Wayne has died. Do you just want to give an English view on that?" and I said "Yes, I think he was probably the last American male" the programme was then inundated with howls of protest. But John Wayne represented a deep gutsy boldness that they just don't have any more in America. It has all got too slick, well packaged and too soft and easy. The presentation seems to be more important than the package itself and that is dangerous! You go through the same procedures of packaging and presentation whatever the product. The principles that apply are the same whether the message, or whatever, is worth hearing or not.

'I cannot package something that I don't believe in, which is why I could never do this for the Labour Party. In Hawaii I was doing seven hours of live radio each day but I needed to earn a bit of extra money. I finished work in the early afternoon and so I got a job as a door-to-door salesman. I was pushing photographs of babies! I would knock on the door of a new mother (we watched the births columns in the newspapers) and try to persuade her that she should have professional photos of her baby taken over the first two years, all presented in a lovely album. They would have photos taken every three months and pay two hundred dollars for the privilege. But my heart wasn't in it, I was going round to all these innocent mothers who had just got home with their babies and trying to sell them photos which really they could take themselves. I just didn't believe in it. It's great to have photos, Marlies and I take them of Leah all the time but why pay two hundred dollars for something you can do yourself? Two hundred dollars was then, in 1963, and still is, a lot of money. I gave it up. I can't sell what I don't believe in!

'If the people, the product or the message are inadequate, then however good the packaging, the failure will show through. If you put a slide in a slide projector, you can do all sorts of things: put it in focus, set it properly on the screen, turn down the lights so that everyone can see it and connect up a sound track but you *cannot project a slide that isn't in the projector*! That is what PR is like, it's a matter of presenting and focusing rather than trying to create a false image.'

Harvey had learned his marketing and communicating skills from the experts and now he came to Europe where most organisations were still amateurs in communications. The Conservative Party like the Church and most groups that work from conviction, had little experience of professional communications. It was believed, and still is by many, that if the message is firm enough, if it is (to them) self evidently right; then people will flock to hear and accept it, simply because of the power and force of that message. Hence the Conservative Party's campaigning did not develop a wide PR strategy until the arrival of Gordon Reece in the mid 1970s.

'Politicians think that people are actually listening to them so they don't try very hard to improve their image. They have this funny idea that enough four syllable words repeated often will automatically get the message across – especially when they are preceded by "As I said in the House of Commons last week . . ."'

'Working on the conferences has been rewarding in that we have managed to progress from that to an awareness of the whole concept of presentation and professionalism. But there are still people who want to do without the Press. They still say to me things to the effect that the media are a nuisance and that we mustn't give way to them too much. That is a very out of date attitude and would be disastrous in the next General Election campaign. People today have a much shorter concentration span that they did ten years ago, which is why ninety per cent. of the paper and bumph that we put out is useless because it's ignored.'

Harvey maintains that politicians are past masters at trotting out political cliches which he would love to eliminate – but he doesn't have much hope. Not only do politicians assume too often that people are actually interested in what they are saying when they are not, they often fail to make what *is* said even half comprehensible. Political cliches, says Harvey, are the enemy of good communication and frequently have a real meaning all of their own. For example:

'The fact of the matter is . . .' means 'Oh dear, I forgot to tell anyone what I was doing and now the other lot has got the initiative and now nobody has the foggiest idea what is going on.' Or:

'You've got to understand . . .' which means 'Why on earth do I have to explain it, isn't it perfectly clear to this moron?'

Cliches and jargon fight the communicators and their attempts to present the case in an interesting, human and sensitive way.

'At the last election a Conservative Party candidate was canvassing for himself in an inner city constituency. He knocks on the door of a seventh floor flat in a tower block on a council estate. He knocks quite persistently and finally the door is opened by a man dressed only in a towel, cigarette dangling from his mouth and shaving soap all over his face, getting ready for his night shift. The candidate looked at him and said "Oh I am sorry,

56

I didn't realise you were changing for dinner!" It would be hysterical if it wasn't true!'

Presentation attitudes and techniques lagged behind the professional PR approach, usually approached with mild hostility. Innovation was often viewed with suspicion, even though in some cases Harvey felt it was not innovation that was required but transfer, for the rest of the world had been using such techniques for years.

'In 1985, technology provides the communicator with an ever expanding range of tools that can enable faster, more natural and more effective communication. The autocue is one such tool. Autocue Ltd, developed the teleprompter we used twenty-five years ago but until very recently it has been the Americans who have made best use of it. With the correct positioning in a large conference hall, the right lighting and an operator who is concentrating, it can enable a speaker to deliver a speech and have eye-contact with the audience, with confidence and authority. The speaker does not have to worry about losing his place in notes because the correct line is always on the screen in front – reflected on a one-way mirror from a TV set on the floor.'

However effective such tools may seem in retrospect, even the simplest (far less sophisticated than the autocue) provoked opposition.

'At conferences it would be sensible to have an electronic adjustable-height lectern. At such conferences the audience wants to see the main speakers and the speaker needs a lectern at the right height. I needed a lectern that could go down to table-top height when the guest on the platform was listening to the debate and which could be raised automatically to the speaker's level when a speech was being given. The lectern needed to be adjustable to suit each individual's needs. For Mrs

Thatcher, I have the front of the lectern thirty-nine inches off the ground. Others have it higher or lower.

'Believe it or not, it took three years of persuasion to get the different politicians to agree even to try this 'monster'. Finally I designed a lectern with some carpenters and engineers and we built it and set it up at a Brighton conference. It was to be operated by the Conference Secretary, Alan Smith, sitting near the speaker where he could see the lectern. It was very basic: a button for 'up' and a button for 'down'. Then we found that a senior politician still objected to it. He said "You'll frighten everybody with it leaping up and down like that." I said "It won't leap up and down, it just goes up or down when the speaker stands or sits."

' "You didn't consult me on it!" he said when we spoke together privately.

' "And you don't consult me on your policies!" I said I could make sure, if left to do it, that he and his colleagues would look good, sound good and be presented well.

'He finally agreed to try it and, of course, the next day everything went smoothly. To give him his due, he came up to me afterwards in front of others and very graciously said "You were right Harvey, it was probably just pre-speech nerves." '

Implementing such changes was neither an easy nor a speedy process. Harvey had been working with the party since January 1978. The bursary that he had received from Andrew Rowe had been increased to an invitation to remain with Conservative Central Office on a full-time basis as Public Relations and Special Projects Consultant. After the 1979 General Election Harvey turned down the opportunity to return to America, to stay on and 'help'. Lord Thorneycroft was one of the people responsible for persuading Harvey to stay on

58

and who made a strong impression on his developing conservatism.

'He is a great man. In the first meeting I spoke for the Tories, he was in the Chair and I remember him saying "Image is what you are, you can't create a false one." '

Harvey did not however, respond to the suggestion by others that he make a speaking tour for the Conservatives during their 1979 campaign. Harvey is a professional speaker and political candidates are usually not. As a professional communicator, he felt it would be tactless to accept the invitation, tempting though it was. In PR, care has to be taken when combining platform speakers. One person who may be a perfectly adequate speaker can have his or her case destroyed by the wrong combinations of status or even personality. Harvey cites one case which he avoided for his own sake.

'While I was working for the Billy Graham Association I got a call from a clergyman friend of mine in Florida. He was pastor of a large and prestigious church. "Harvey" he said. "We'd like you to say a word in the morning service when you're here"

' "Fine," I said.

' "Look," he went on. "Here's what we're going to do. The President (Nixon) will be there and he's going to say a few words and then your boss (Billy Graham) will be with us too and he's going to say a word or two and we thought . . .

' "No way!" I said. There's a time to shut up and no way would I follow those two!'

Harvey has never considered going into politics himself.

'I feel I can do most for the Conservative cause in communications. When you have worked extensively internationally, you realise how the world fits together and how much we can benefit from knowing more about one another, rather than closing the doors around our own country.

'I remember in New Guinea there was a woman feeding a baby on one breast and a small pig on the other. Although it's not something we would do, it's perfectly logical. If the mother has milk and the pig needs it, why not? They need the pig to grow and be healthy. When you have had a wide experience of the world it is impossible to limit your thinking to one country. On that basis the only elected post I might think about would be the European Parliament, although the MPs there are pretty powerless at the moment. All the same I think it will grow, because countries have to cross international barriers.'

International barriers have come to mean little to Harvey in his travels through ninety-seven countries. A knowledge of the international scene and his observations of the way other cultures approach problems has left him feeling that the British have a lot to learn, not only in the field of communications but in more general areas.

'The Church in particular, tends to look at the falling attendances and say "We hold services at eleven in the morning and six in the evening and nobody comes." No one ever seems to ask the obvious question "How do we get people into Church?" Perhaps we should dispense with the regular services.

'In America that's how they approach a problem. Instead of saying impotently "We always do it this way". They say "We've got a problem, how do we solve it?" It is a more specific and logical approach, starting from scratch, not excluding any course of action. It is not hampered by tradition or preconceived ideas about what is "always done".

'When I first came to Conservative Central Office, I was able to get a new digital PBX telephone exchange

60

installed, to replace the one that had been there for years – just because I knew how and where to go to *find* the information and what to do with it when I found it.

'It was this approach to a problem that kept me relaxed in human terms while I was buried under the rubble in Brighton. I knew that the problem (my predicament) could be solved, if not by me, by the firemen. I knew too that I must breathe to deal with the problem. All I had to do was keep quiet and calm.'

8: Introducing Luis Palau!

'Extraordinarily I never thought about fire. I don't know how I would have reacted if I had thought of it! There was no fire because all the gas appliances were on the ground floor or below. The Grand Hotel was not a modern hotel and did not have kitchens and breakfast rooms in the higher floors.

'Neither have I suffered from shock, then or later in the day or in the months that followed. It would be quite *wrong* to say that I was brave. I was not hurt, unlike others buried in the rubble and I was not in serious pain. I could feel all my body, I had no broken bones. None of my limbs were bent in the wrong direction. I knew that fundamentally I was all right and this helped me to relax while I waited for help. I also knew that Marlies was safe in London and for that I was especially thankful, it helped me to relax while I waited.

'It was about an hour before I heard anything other than the firebells, which just went on and on, that and the water. I wish someone could have switched those bells off. But above them I heard voices. At first some people calling to others who were buried to help them, I could not hear their replies but I called out for help. I couldn't get much air in my lungs because of the weight of the masonry on my chest but I did think that I had yelled loudly, although it soon became clear that I had not been heard. So I yelled again, this time with all the air and power I could muster and I heard a man say. "There's someone alive in there!" They started to come in my direction and called back "Shout again! Shout again! where are you?". From then on I began this conversation with two firemen Mick Ayling and Ken Towner. They were not only very brave and professional people, they were great PR men. I knew as I lay there that they were *making* me shout, they kept talking to me. They were not to know that I was not badly hurt, they had to assume that I was and so they kept talking to establish where I was and to keep my morale up. Even so I could hear snatches of rather less encouraging conversations.

"Get a safety line over there!"

"I can't, there's too big a gap!"

"Watch that drop it's five floors down!"

"Mind those cables!" Not only had the explosion fractured the water tanks but it had sheared the electricity cables and they were swinging overhead, arcing in the pouring water.

'It was very dangerous for them out there, I had no idea that I was insulated from the electricity and I didn't know that the pile of rubble I was in was ready to fall at any moment. That was why they could not use lifting gear because they could not get a safe purchase on the rubble. They were marvellous, they did an excellent job.'

Fireman Mick Ayling was the one who had identified just where Harvey was positioned. When the firemen had been called out that night, they had been apprehensive as to what they would find. When they arrived, everything was quiet.

'There wasn't a sound to begin with, not even glass. The only things we could hear were the fire alarms ringing, even the seagulls had not been disturbed, or else they'd gone. It looked as though it was foggy or smoky but actually it was dust.'

When they arrived, at first they went round the back and then Mick was detailed to go up the front of the building. He did so and went in through the first floor window. He went through the room and turned right into the corridor only to discover Mrs Thatcher and others, still not sure of what had happened. They, of course, were soon taken care of, escorted carefully off the premises by the police, while Mick went up to what he guessed was the fourth floor. There he was told that there were people somewhere, but that they couldn't locate them. It was then that Harvey called out 'I'm here, I'm here!'

'Where are you?' shouted Mick.

'I'm here! Here!' Mick started to climb about on the rubble, but that increased the pressure on Harvey who responded quickly with 'Be careful! Be careful!' Mick adjusted his approach.

'What's your name?' he called.

'Harvey, Harvey Thomas'

'Well we'll call you Harvey!'

'Then, all of a sudden it went quiet,' Mick recalls and they all yelled 'Oy come on! Come on keep talking!'

Harvey did notice that the firemen went to some effort to keep him talking and while they called out among themselves they talked to him. The cables flashed and crackled a little distance from them and their perch was unsteady. 'If you stood up and relaxed, you'd have gone down three floors.' To prevent the consequences of that Mick was roped together with another fireman Ken Towner, at first with sheets, later with rope.

When Ken Towner had arrived at the scene he was told to go straight up into the building which he did. He went up a fire escape on the front of the hotel and he too noticed the sounds in the aftermath of the explosion.

'The first thing I remember is the firebells and there

Above: Harvey aged two ... and at seventeen.

Below: Harvey in action for Luis Palau at QPR.

Above: a recent photograph of Harvey.

Above: Mrs Marlies Thomas.

Below: a week after the bomb, as a member of Mrs. Thatcher's constituency, Harvey attended the celebration of her 25th year as MP for Finchley.

Right: an aerial view of the devastated Grand Hotel Brighton the morning after the IRA bomb exploded.

Below: firemen dig in the debris to find Harvey.

Above: the centre of the hotel is ripped out by the force of the blast. Harvey's bed was in the centre of the top room, immediately over the bomb.

Below: a photograph showing Harvey's approximate position when he was rescued.

was lots of pouring water coming from the fractured tanks above us.

'I met Mick on the fifth floor, and we identified more or less where Harvey was. We could see his face (just about) there was this half moon shape visible and Mick cleared the rubble away from his eyes and face. Harvey complained mainly about the pressure on his legs and chest. He was well buried and could hardly move at all.'

Ken had come up to the fifth floor with a group of firemen and once he had assessed the situation, he told them what equipment he wanted and several of them went off to get it. Ken goes to some trouble to point out that although it was Mick and himself who spoke to Harvey and dug out the rubble closest to him, they were not on their own.

'Behind us was a team of about eighteen to twenty firemen. They were all getting equipment and moving stuff out of the way. Mick went forward first because there was only room for one of us to work next to Harvey, so he passed bits of rubble to me and I passed it on to the men behind me. I suggested that we be roped together in some way because where we were, beneath us there was just a hole, we could see right down to the road below.

'We started talking to him, and I remember that Harvey said he had been praying a lot and I appreciated that. He told us about Marlies and the baby they were expecting and he thanked God that he was a survivor.

'We told him that it had been a bomb, there was no point in holding it back from him. We had to keep him talking because, at the time, we didn't know how badly hurt he was, also the water was making him cold. When I got there I took most of the water on myself, I caught it on my helmet and sort of guided it away from him. We did rig up some sort of sheeting but that cut down the light we had to work by.'

It was not only cold for Ken but also for Harvey and

it was to be another hour-and-a-half before he could be pulled free from his tottering tower of rubble.

Even though he had now committed himself to work for the Conservative Party, and had accepted and was to experience the risks involved in such a commitment, Harvey had not deserted his first vocation of setting up evangelistic crusades. He put in a full day's work for the Conservatives but it was agreed that he could do additional consultancies using his own private office in North London.

One additional consultancy project, a voluntary effort, was with Luis Palau, an Argentinian born evangelist who is often seen as a successor to Billy Graham.

'I first met Luis Palau on a crusade with Billy Graham, in Baton Rouge, Louisiana. I was with Billy in his room just before an evening meeting and Luis came in. Billy said to me "Harvey, I want you to meet Luis Palau. I believe God is going to give him the burden of world evangelism that our Team has been carrying since the Second World War." '

'I met Luis next in Spain in 1974 at the Iberian Congress on Evangelism. Luis was born an Argentinian but for twenty years now he has lived in Portland, Oregon. I warmed to him enough then to want to persuade the relevant committee that he should speak at Eurofest '75 in Brussels. The Programme Committee for Eurofest were reluctant at first to the idea of Luis being a main speaker. It was to be a ten day event and that meant ten morning addresses, a lot to offer someone they hardly knew. I finally persuaded them to alternate two speakers over the ten days, Bishop Festo Kivengere and Luis Palau so that they each had five messages to give. The result was marvellous, because they each gave fantastic addresses which were completely different in approach. The Bishop is a man of great stature and he delivered his sermons with dignity and depth. Luis was more flamboyant and he appealed to the young people who came from all over Europe. He dealt with subjects that had never been tackled openly before. I remember the horror of my colleagues when he said "Now if you want to go to bed with someone what are you going to do about it?" Before he came along we used to pretend that sex didn't exist for the Christian, but he tackled it head on. His approach did provoke some opposition at the time but most of it has melted away since.

'It was in Spain that I first told Luis that he should come to England. He replied that he came to preach in Spain regularly but that he had never been to England. I said that I would be prepared to set up meetings for him because I believed that we needed his minstry in the UK. So in 1976 I travelled round the country contacting people I knew and who knew me through my work for Billy Graham saying "There's a man called Luis Palau, I'd like to bring him over here and I'd like you to host a rally for him." Of course most people replied:

' "Loueese who?" but we set up several successful rallies some of which were then followed by major crusades.'

Just as in politics in England there has been little respect for Public Relations, so the Church has found it difficult to understand the need or use for it. The Church is so often associated with amateurish presentation but sometimes this can be quite endearing. Harvey remembers one incident in Cardiff when Luis was speaking at an early rally there.

'It was a hot summer's night in July 1976 and it was one of these Baptist Chapels with rows of hard wooden pews. In an attempt to renovate the Church and give it a smarter face, they had just varnished all the pews but it hadn't dried! That, combined with all the heat meant that the platform party stuck to their seats.'

Such an incident is an amusing example of presen-

67

tation which hasn't quite come up to twentieth century standards. Like politicians, they believe their opinions to be self-evidently true and therefore they do not need any 'hype' to put the message across to the public; the unfailing truth of the message should be enough. Falling attendances suggest otherwise, so when Mission to London came to the capital in 1984, with Luis Palau as its spearhead, Harvey brought into action the professional might of Gallup Polls and an agency advertising campaign. Churches had long since been putting up posters for their events but now was the time to find out what type of poster would really appeal to the "man in the street".

Anyone who visited London in the summer of 1984 would have seen the results of that research. The tubes, buses and streets were witness to a remarkable advertising campaign. A striking black-and-white poster of a fairly ordinary, benign looking man, sitting in a large leather armchair, or perhaps standing behind it with a book in his hand. Sometimes he leant on the back of it facing the viewer. This was a personality who had something to say. The book was a heavy hint. The slogans were clear but not clumsy "Bring your doubts" and "Take this Bus to QPR where Luis Palau will take you further". Underneath, in smaller type, was the explanation that this was an invitation to hear the Christian message.

'At first it was hard to convince the Mission to London team that if we announced "a Crusade for Christ" or something similar, and suggested that people had a responsibility to come to it for their own good, there would be no response. The Church has this tendency to keep re-inventing the wheel. I had a great sense of déjà vu sometimes, because the principles we had learnt over twenty years of international crusades were not always being implemented in this one. We had learnt, even at

68

Maine Road Stadium in 1961, that the appeal of the preacher as a personality was fading. People wouldn't just come to be preached at, as they had once flocked to hear Spurgeon or Wesley. We needed to give people more reason to come. That was the first time, in the UK, when we used "Operation Andrew", the teaching in John 1 verses forty to forty-two "Andrew went to find his brother Peter and brought him to Jesus" A Christian asks a friend to come with them to a crusade.

'I wasn't all that popular but the Committee, led by a great servant of God, Gilbert Kirby, were very patient with me and we got over our reservations by commissioning a Gallup survey, an extensive in-depth qualitative survey of seven major areas of London. Gallup personnel sat down with people and showed them photographs of Luis and asked them to respond. For example we showed them a photograph of Luis with his hands outstretched and although they had not seen Luis before, they replied "That man's a preacher" But the moment any *words* were with the photo, for instance "This is Luis Palau, come and hear him" or "Luis Palau has a message for you" their attitude changed from "He's a preacher" to "He's a con-man, he's phoney" and they did not trust him.

'We also learned, that most people *think* of themselves as Christians. They do not like to be told that they are not Christians. They live in a Christian culture and therefore they are Christians. Born again believers would say otherwise but that direct accusation would, of course, be resented. So, we couldn't put on the poster, "Come and be converted" or even "Come and hear the Christian message".

'We had to be more subtle and less offensive to those we wanted to reach. It was these results that guided the advertisers "The Sales Promotion Agency" a subsidiary of Saatchi and Saatchi. They did their job superbly.

The results did create controversy and division in the committee.

'They came up with the slogans "Bring Your doubts" and "Take the tube/bus to QPR where Luis Palau will take you further". We put the Christian message on the poster but the whole Mission was organised so that people would already know *who* Luis Palau was and the photos should also have given a hint as to what it was about.

'We had planned that the advertising campaign would *support* the work of local Christians in the city. As it turned out it had a much greater impact than we had expected. Each night at Queens Park Rangers stadium Luis would ask the crowd who had come *just because* of the advertising campaign and as many as fifteen to twenty five per cent. would raise their hands. The campaign was so obviously successful that early reservations disappeared.

'Not all aspects of the crusade were as successful as we had hoped. Mission to London took place over two years in two phases. The advertising was intended to be the culmination of the second phase: to provide the right climate for Christians to invite their friends to QPR. We made a significant mistake in having too large a "first phase" in 1983. We had a number of local rallies to which churchgoers brought their friends. This was the "Operation Andrew" approach, the intention was to enable people to get to know Luis and it was this phase that won many people for the Lord.

'It was hoped that the people who had come to the local rallies would be so keen that they would come to QPR, bring their friends and arrange coach trips for larger groups from their churches.

'However it is a basic principle that you can only have one major goal. There can only be one Cup Final each year. There is only one Wimbledon. To try and have

70

two major crusades in the same twelve months was a mistake. Many people came to Christ and I thank God for that but we cut down the impact of QPR because too many people who would have worked for it had put all their energy into the first phase and we had to make major and last minute efforts to get Christians to make a second great sacrifice of time and bring their friends to QPR. There was an average attendance of six thousand a night but I believe this could have been doubled – with the resulting increase in souls saved – if the churches had only been asked to make *one* sacrificial effort instead of two. They simply did not have the resources to give many months in two consecutive years.

'When I listened to Billy in Sheffield in June 1985 I noticed the strength of support he had gathered from *both* the mainstream denominations and the charismatic and house group fellowships.

'In his crusades so far in Europe, Luis Palau has not had enough support from the mainstream denominations.

'I believe that Luis Palau is called by God to continue the wide international ministry of Billy Graham but to do so he will need the huge mainstream sector (albeit often apathetic) of the Christian Church.'

9: Interest, Inform, Involve

'I bear no personal bitterness towards the people who set the bomb. I was conscious, lying under the rubble, of the thought that in God's eyes, they were no more than fallen men, without salvation. As Christians we're so good at being spiritual and telling each other how good we are, that we often fail to tell people the good news. We're supposed to tell everybody the gospel of Christ. If we were succeeding, perhaps there would be no terrorists. That's why I feel it is important for Christians and the Church as a whole to evangelise. We *have* to communicate the Gospel. From time to time special stimulation and encouragement by the local church and united crusades – well planned and with sufficient prayer support – can meet that need.

'In the same way (in secular terms) politicians need to put over their philo sophy and communicate their message constantly, with something special in the strategy occasionally.

'The problem with communications in both these spheres, is that we tend to try and get people *involved* in working for us before we have either *interested* them or *informed* them. The Church insists that people come to Church services at set times. Then, if they do come they are bored stiff. No wonder people feel they would rather clean the car on a Sunday or go shopping. Maybe if the

Church really has to compete on a Sunday, it might be forced into presenting its message more dynamically.

'Three basic words outline the principles of Public Relations and effective communications 'interest', 'inform' and 'involve' – *in that order*! Too often Christians and politicians try to communicate their respective messages by attempting to get people *'involved'* first, then *'informing'* them and then *'interesting'* them. A politician knocks on the door and asks "Will you vote for me?" That's asking them to get *involved* before they have got *interested*. In the same way the Church wants people to act like Christians and to come to Church before they have even caught their interest. Having a good reason *why* is not enough these days because it is not always clear to those you want to reach. With the right approach, it is possible to interest people in anything – especially Jesus Christ, salvation and political philosophy. You're not supposed to discuss religion or politics in 'company' – why I don't know. For real people talking real language they're two of the most fascinating topics.

'I saw a newspaper advertisement which was an example of the right way to communicate. There was a photograph of a boy and a girl standing facing one another, with various words written over the pictures. The word at the top, which attracts attention, was 'impotence'. Immediately your *interest* is caught and you read right through. It's a very clever advertisement, in this case it was about drugs and what they do to you. After catching your *interest* with the slogan, they then *inform* you, telling the reader about the danger of drugs and then at last there is a form that you can fill in, to get more information or donate or whatever; that is the point at which you start to get *involved*.

'To get your message across you must *interest* the people first, no one will get *involved* in anything if they're not *interested* in it. This was the principle used in Mission to London with Luis Palau.'

Conviction and enthusiasm, Harvey maintains come from interest, followed by information, only *then* can you become committed enough to want to join in. 'Conviction' in this sense means the knowledge that something is right! The inner satisfaction that a belief is real. Conviction in the evangelical world often has another meaning. 'Being convicted' has a meaning, more like a legal phrase. Just as a man may be convicted of murder a person may become 'Convicted' of their sin, only this time the awareness of guilt comes from within the individual and not from the law. 'Conviction' in the evangelical sense means that an individual has realised that he or she is a sinner in need of salvation. God offers that salvation only through faith in Christ and his death and resurrection. Conviction of sin can thus lead to 'conviction' in the more secular sense and the conviction that the Gospel is true and vital. Both those forms of conviction lead to involvement and commitment to Christ.

It is the awareness of conviction in both senses that Harvey feels is necessary in the Church today. He feels that parts of the Church and some of its leaders have lost that conviction.

'It was back in Northwestern Bible College that I really felt convinced of the Church's prime ministry. I didn't go into the Christian ministry myself and become a pastor because I didn't feel called to but if I *had* gone into it, then my responsibility would be almost exclusively spiritual, to win souls for the Lord, to teach the Bible and to have an evangelistic ministry. I would, as a minister, have a recognition of the world's problems and perhaps, as an individual have got involved. But as a minister of the Church I would have to put first the winning of some of the fifty million or so people in the

74

United Kingdom who do not know Christ as personal saviour. The Bible says "Seek ye *first* the Kingdom of God and His righteousness". When *hearts* are changed, social and political problems become a lot easier to solve. When I see some of the naïve political rubbish waffled out today by people who pretend to be Christian leaders and the ignoring of human needs by others, I am reminded of the man who bought a 1985 Lotus Special car. He went to a Baptist and then a Congregational Minister to ask them to give a blessing on it.

' "I'd be glad to" they each replied "but what is a Lotus Special?" He went away in disgust to an unmentionable Bishop with the same request.

' "So you've got a Lotus Special" the Bishop said. "Lead me to it, I want a ride in it – by the way, what's a blessing?"

'The Bible says it is the prime responsibility of a minister to preach the Gospel and only *with that Gospel* to meet social problems. Not because those problems are not important but because of the meaning of the verse "Seek ye *first* the Kingdom of God and all these things will be added unto you" . . . If we seek the will of God first then other things *will* sort themselves out. That's why it's important that a minister should preach the Gospel and uphold the faith.

'I get embarrassed today when I hear some people who purport to be Christian ministers and who even go under the title of Bishop and yet who do not believe in the Bible. Such people do not meet the Biblical qualifications for Christian leadership and they have a long way to go before any constituency would select them as a parliamentary candidate.'

It is the lack of that commitment that Harvey believes is largely responsible for falling attendances. Not only does the Church seem unable to present itself well but many times it is unsure of what it wants to present. In an attempt to present a better image to the public, its leaders have watered down the message. A trivial example of this is the method of modernising language; changing the great hymn "Thine be the glory" to "Yours be the glory". The Church need not be ashamed of archaic language where it communicates as it does so effectively in the original wording of that hymn. The more modern version simply dilutes the old version and takes away its impact. In the same way there is no need to dilute the message of Christ, to make it more palatable. It's no use creating something more presentable if it isn't true! The problem is how to present the message we already have, not how to change the message!

A dull, lifeless service can make any truth seem uninteresting. Harvey points out that the truth of the gospel message is not watered down in the crusades, nor is the language of the hymns changed and yet the people come and the young people in tens of thousands.

It's quite true that the people come to hear the message and to sing the songs but one way of interesting them is to bring in a celebrity to entertain and build up to the communication of the verbal message.

'In 1979 I was beginning to feel that it was the time to start introducing show business celebrities and the like into some rallies for the Conservative Party. This has been done in America for years. The Billy Graham Team would often invite a Christian personality to sing or give a testimony at a crusade to get people interested. Cliff Richard is an example of that happening over here. In America there were Dale Evans and Roy Rogers and others. So in 1979 at the Conservative Trade Unionist election rally we invited a few sympathetic personalities to come and join us. All of them were trade unionists in their profession, so it wasn't a gimmick as such, they were all legitimately involved in the unions. Some of them have suffered in their careers since. They have been told "If you're with the Conservatives, you're on your way out."

'For the first time we introduced a Master of Ceremonies, rather than a "Chairman" of the meeting. The MC in that case was Dick Tracey, now an MP. We had music too, Gordon Reece adapted the words of "Hello Dolly" to "Hello Maggie" and we planned entrances of the Party Leaders carefully. We let the entertainment happen and then we changed the focus on stage, and therefore the meeting, to concentrate on the entry of Mrs Thatcher. She wasn't hidden behind a top table with people in front of her. At that rally the crowd was going to see the next Prime Minister properly.

'As she came on somebody in the audience shouted "What about the song?". They yelled it just as Sir Fred Hardman was going to introduce her.

'It was one of those moments when, as producer, you know that you have captured the audience. Sometimes professionally, you just know when something is right, when something is going to work. Even though it wasn't in the programme or planned at all I put my hand on Lulu's back and said "Lulu the song!". Earlier that evening I had said to both the sound man and the organist "All you have to do tonight is watch me!" and, bless them, they both did.

'I pointed to the microphone that Lulu was going to use for the sound man to switch it on and I signalled the organist. Fred Hardman turned to her and Lulu was singing "Hello Maggie" with the whole audience joining in. Mrs Thatcher, who responds marvellously to people, went over to Lulu and they linked arms – it was quite an introduction! It was my old friend Andrew Rowe with Gordon Reece who had the courage to go ahead with this approach.'

Harvey's contribution on the Conservative's new-look did not go unnoticed. After that particular rally "Time

Magazine" remarked that if anyone had noticed a certain revivalist feeling to the meeting they would not be surprised to know that its producer had once been with the Billy Graham Team.

The hallmark of that campaign in the General Election of 1979 was not just the fervour and life in the rallies but the whole approach to communications and advertising prepared by Gordon Reece and Saatchi and Saatchi.

'The very fact that we still talk about the 1979 campaign shows how effective it was. Gordon Reece pioneered a new attitude to campaigning and advertising in British politics. It was designed to present the message and the politicans well enough to win the hearts of the people – and it did. Of course some of the political traditionalists were appalled but then they would be!'

Personal presentation has been an uphill struggle in politics as it is in the Church. Harvey has been conducting television training tutorials for politicians not only from the UK but from other parts of the world who want to present a better face to the public.

'Television, like any communication is a very personal medium. Most of the time you see a person from a distance of about three feet and you can only see the head and shoulders. You can't lecture or pronounce pompously on television. This is the great failure of many people in front of the camera. They tend to stiffen up and they think they've got to look frightfully "propah". The only time that most people think of dandruff is when they see themselves on the video monitor. A man will sit terribly stiff and upright. They don't understand that the principles of communication are naturalness, genuiness, normality. You don't put it on! Jargon and waffle are the enemies of communication.

'The first thing I do in a session is my own "piece to camera" (where I face the camera and record my own

78

talk) about fifteen minutes long, outlining the basic principles. I try to underline that you don't put it on, you don't sit there as if you're talking to millions of people. You're not talking to millions of people. You're talking to the interviewer, the cameraman and a couple of people in their own front room. So the medium is very personal, it's really a part of a fireside chat.

'The next thing I say is that you always look at the person to whom you are speaking. You're having a conversation with him and the people at home are listening in. Sometimes the interviewer is "down-the-line", that is geographically he is somewhere away from you so you talk to the camera because the camera has become the eyes of the interviewer.

'You don't have to worry too much about the microphone or the lighting, all that will be dealt with for you. You will do a voice check so that the sound engineer can adjust the levels to balance your voice properly with the voice and volume of the other speakers and the rest of the programme. When you do a voice test, speak at your normal level. It's often worth sitting in the studio lights for a while before you record or transmit, so that you can get used to the intensity. It is always difficult for Mrs Thatcher to come into a hall with floodlights from an ordinary room. Other speakers have a chance to adjust to the lighting while they listen to a debate but the Prime Minister goes "straight on" which is much more difficult.

When it comes to what to wear, don't wear black and white! You'll look like a penguin. Avoid very bright colours. White and gaudy colours reflect back the light and the subsequent glare can make you appear to glow. Stripes and checks tend to 'strobe' or move in the light and that can be distracting. Try not to wear jewellery or fussy things round your neck, all those things detract from you and what you have to say.

A crucial thing, not just on television but in any kind of public communication, is to do everything deliberately. Don't look at your notes surreptitiously. If you need to look, look deliberately. If you need to blow your nose, turn away from the mike (to save the sound engineer's ears) get out your handkerchief and blow. Apologise and get back to the interview. If you do anything in an embarrassed manner, your embarrassment will be communicated. It's like watching Torvill and Dean on ice slipping just slightly and then recovering. You're embarrassed for them and you catch your breath. But when the clown in "Holiday on Ice" comes on and constantly seems to be falling you laugh with him and you're not embarrassed because you know he's doing it deliberately.

'Once all that is established you must use language that is simple and easy to understand because you're talking to Mr and Mrs Bloggs (if they will allow me) in Burnley or Sheffield or Wapping or the Bronx. It's no use trying to impress your political colleagues. The people who need to have the message communicated to them are sitting at home.

'Politicians really do think that people are listening to what they are saying. They don't realise that it's not words that they communicate but attitude. People are 'listening' to the look on the face, the tone in the voice, the expression in the eyes, not the actual words first.

'Posture is important. Make sure that you're not looking down your nose at the interviewer because you'll also be looking down your nose at at the viewer.

'You'd better know your stuff too. I remember once doing a mock interview with a candidate for the European Parliament who had already been a member for four years and he did not know that the rebate we were owed by the EEC had not been paid. He was convinced that it had. That kind of gap in your knowledge will be ruthlessly exposed by an astute interviewer.

'Once I've explained all this, I put my client through a gruelling political interview. I do my homework on these people. I get researchers to come up with information on them and their subject and I make the interview as difficult as I can.

Then we go through it, frame by frame and discuss how they responded and how they appear to the viewer. Most of them are good about it but it can be a very humiliating experience. Some try to defend every inflection. They say "Oh but I said that because I knew that such and such was the case". My reply is:

"But Mrs Bloggs in Burnley doesn't know that!" The subject must also be genuine. Any falsity will show.

'I usually do a second interview. This is an easy "early evening" type interview. It's about them as a person, their personality, the things they like to do in their spare time and their family. Then we go through that interview and try and apply some of the more relaxed approach to the first interview.

'I remember once a senior politician telling me that he had done on radio, an interview which he thought was useless. All they had talked about was his hobby of gardening and the fact that he was building a wall in his garden. To his surprise he got more letters about that interview than from any of his other interviews of a more political nature.

'Practicalities to be aware of in a TV studio! Don't drink, don't smoke, get used to the lights, don't walk away before the interview's finished and be aware that microphones and cameras run before and after the interview itself.

'Once when Mrs Thatcher had an interview on Panorama she made a very minor mistake, she called Sir Robin Day "Mr Day". When the interview was over a colleague came up to her and said. "Fine interview Prime Minister but did you realise that you stripped Sir Robin of his title?" She replied:

"Did I? Oh I'm so sorry." To which Sir Robin Day replied. "Yes, Prime Minister nine times."

'The cameras and sound were still running and that night the national news carried hardly anything about the interview but plenty about that little personal item.

'Having said that, the use of President Reagan's comments about "bombing Russia" I consider to be entirely unprofessional. He did what we all do when we're testing microphones. He made a few joking comments. My usual one at a Party Conference is to say "Ladies and gentlemen please make sure you're firmly strapped into your seats, just in case the person next to you wakes up!" Those sorts of comments are not meant for public use nor are they meant to be taken seriously, they're just a bit of fun.

'After the training, it is not always easy to see the results. Ideally it would be best to have one session a week for some time but that would be a full-time job.'

Communication at its most effective is often not the result of training but of trauma, when the subject is stripped of inhibitions. Harvey recalls that when he was asked to answer press questions after the bombing, because he was the only one around, he was dishevelled, dirty, he had only a blanket round him and he wasn't really aware of the massed ranks of the press hidden behind banks of TV lighting. As a result he was totally uninhibited when telling his story.

It is the aim of all professional communicators, that people with a message be able to communicate it effectively. Sometimes it is particularly in the extremity of a crisis like the bombing of the Grand Hotel, that professionals like Mrs Thatcher communicate with a power and reality that few can ignore.

10: Berlin '81

'Which way are you facing? the firemen asked.

'When I went to bed I think I was facing north to south.' replied Harvey.

'Well we think you're facing east to west now.'

'I was busy keeping alive because, by this time, my air was running out. The water which was pouring through the rubble was blocking the gaps through which fresh air could come. As the firemen got nearer they explained what they were doing. They kept saying "Can you see the light Harvey?" (apparently they had a torch).

"I saw the Light long ago brother but I can't see yours yet." I called back. Soon after that, they found my head, "Where's the rest of you?"

"Straight down from my chin" I replied. Then a man called out that he was a doctor.

"Harvey, can you answer some questions?" He went through the list of things that would indicate my state to the firemen and the doctor. Could I feel my left hand, my right hand, my left leg, my right leg? Was I in any pain? Did I want a painkiller? I replied to his last question that although the pressure of the rubble made it difficult to breathe I didn't want to take anything unless I absolutely had to, I wasn't in that much pain and I knew I was going to get out, so I had great peace of mind.

The fire chief had made one of the firemen take a break and it was only then that I began to realise how long and how hard they had been working. They had had to take the rubble away piece by piece. They couldn't get any lifting gear near me because my position was so precarious, over the five storey drop. They had managed to rig up a tarpaulin over the rubble so that not so much water came down over me but by this time I was very cold. It was October and night time on the Brighton sea front five storeys up. I could feel the cold air coming up from below me. All I was wearing was a T shirt and the sheet that had wrapped itself round my neck.'

It was Mick Ayling who had had to take a break, although not because he was tired, there was not really time for that.

'I cut myself' said Mick. 'I don't how I did it, but it could have been a bit of glass or metal, metal I think, because whatever it was went clattering down. Anyway, I carried on for a bit, but then Harvey suddenly says "Blood, there's blood!". I realised then that I'd better get it seen to, as it was worrying him slightly so I got treatment for it and then came back, I pushed one of the others out the way and we used this air-compressed saw to start cutting through the bedding and some beams.'

For Harvey the sawing was a nerve racking time.

'They began to saw through a beam, I could feel it very close to my leg and I told them so.'

' "It's all right" they said. "it's only an air saw," and I spent a few minutes trying to work out what that was. Could it really be a saw that used air? Of course what they meant was a motor saw but they used that sort of language to keep me happy. Ken Towner had asked for the saw, which worked by compressed air, to be brought in, although they found that hand saws were more useful in the situation.

'We used a compressed air saw called a Cengar, the sort we tend to use in road accidents to cut people out of cars. We told Harvey not to worry, that it was only the air saw. In fact, what he probably didn't know was that we were cutting away from him and not towards his leg, so although he could feel it we were not likely to cut him.'

'Towards the end the weight was getting harder and harder for me to bear, the rubble was growing heavier because it was wet and settling down. It was presenting quite a problem but I was comforted to realise that it was still night and Marlies would not yet have woken up to hear the news.

'I met Marlies at a Conference on evangelism in Lausanne in Switzerland in 1976. We were married on December 22nd 1978. It was six days after the bomb on October 18th 1984 that our daughter, Leah, was born. When we were first married Marlies and I worked together. She is an extraordinarily fast typist and people often comment on her speed at the keyboard. Marlies has sometimes typed the Prime Minister's speeches for the autocue and until Leah's birth she was very involved with my work outside the Conservative Party. She is from Altenkirchen in Germany and has a marvellous family with a Christian Brethren background. Erich and Irene her parents live in a tiny village in the Westerwald. She has two sisters, Ulla and Hanni who are twins.

'One of the more unusual and interesting projects we worked on was the "Jesus '81 Berlin Airlift" in Berlin which was fabulous. It was probably one of the most progressive events I have taken part in. We had thirty-one thousand people in the Berlin Olympic Stadium (the stadium built by Hitler for the 1936 Olympic Games) for one weekend.

'The originator of the idea was Volkhard Spitzer. He has been a pastor of the Christian centre of Berlin (which is by far the biggest Church in Berlin) for some twenty years. He and I have been friends for a long time and he is a great Christian but in the eyes of other German Christians he is not really accepted because he is a Pentecostal.

'In Germany in 1909 a declaration was made in Berlin by the German Evangelicals which stated generally that "Pentecostalism was not from God". If anything it came, in their view, from the Devil. Although I am not Pentecostal I have never doubted that their theology is Bible based and that Volkhard's preaching is fundamentally sound, by any Christian standards. Since 1909, attitudes in Germany, towards the Pentecostals have softened a little, but that edict has never been repealed. The effect of the proclamation has never been fully eradicated and while the Pentecostals generally want to join with the mainstream churches, to evangelise, witness and arrange events together, there is still the feeling from those denominations that the Pentecostals do not quite meet their spiritual standards.

'Peter Schneider, however, who was the General Secretary of the German Evangelical Alliance has always been sympathetic to other Christian denominations. Thus when Volkhard Spitzer came up with the idea of the "Jesus '81, Berlin Airlift" Schneider did not oppose strongly. Volkhard went ahead and asked Marlies and I to help in the setting up of it. We agreed to do so, although by then I was fully involved with the Conservatives and I did wonder where I would find the extra time. I have always found that with projects like that, the Lord does provide the time for us to work and on this occasion we worked over the weekends. We did have to work hard though, there was a committee of six that met once a month in America. This may sound extravagant but when we worked it out, it cost less to get us and the other European committee members over to the States than to rotate our meetings or meet in Europe. It meant that we would retreat stateside on a Friday evening and return some time in the small hours of a Monday morning and go virtually straight in to work. The other weekends in the month were taken up with travel to various European cities, advertising and arranging the event itself.

'There were still problems in Germany though; even with the courtesy of Peter Schneider. The majority of the Evangelical Alliance membership did not want to take part in it. This was partly because when Volkhard had announced the project he had presented it as a Vision from the Lord. This immediately left him open to the accusation that his vision was not from God and that he was claiming a false authority for his idea. Volkhard claimed to have had a Vision of the Berlin Olympic Stadium filled with Christians; the Alliance then said that if he did not fill the stadium this would prove that the Vision was false. The churches of the Alliance therefore tried quite hard to make sure that the Stadium was not full. The Alliance magazine "IDEA" ran an article saying the project was wrong and not "of the Lord" and people should not go. We invited them to attend the event itself as observers. Peter Schneider maintained a very pleasant profile and kept in touch with us and all that was going on.

'When the weekend arrived it did no dishonour to Volkhard's vision. We had thirty thousand people in the Stadium. A good half of them were Germans, which meant that many of them *must* have come from the mainstream churches in West Germany. We had made special flight arrangements for people coming into Berlin from West Germany or from the rest of Europe. We booked many hotel rooms in Berlin, in fact all the hotel bookings were handled on computer and it was the first time a computer had been used in Germany in evangelical circles. There is no problem with getting into Berlin. You can drive through East Germany with your head hanging out of the window singing gospel songs if you want to. You won't be all that popular but no one will harass you.

Our guest speakers, at the weekend, included Paul Yonggi Cho pastor of the world's biggest church (ten thousand members) in Seoul in Korea. We had Pat Boone and the Edwin Hawkins singers and although it kept threatening to rain, it only succeeded once. Out of our seven rallies that weekend, only one had to suffer a ten minute dampening.

We had a woman called Ruth Price, a German Jew. She had survived Auchswitz and had left Germany vowing that she would never return.

She had become a Christian and now she stood in the middle of that Stadium: the stadium built to honour Hitler's Nazism but which witnessed its humiliation. She told the people "I have come back to say to you that Jesus loves you!"

'There was the evangelist Arthur Blessitt too, an American Baptist who has literally taken up his cross and walked. He wanders the world preaching and witnessing, often in the most dangerous situations. He has a large wooden cross, which he carries over his shoulder but which has a wheel on it to make transportation slightly easier.

'His style of preaching is full of spell-binding witness and the people loved his message and his enthusiastic delivery. It is, in a way, sad that Arthur is so spontaneous in his approach because it means that I can never help him very much because I can never tell where he is going to be or when. I have great respect for him

88

because if he believes the Lord is telling him to go somewhere he just goes.

'The officials of the Evangelical Alliance in Germany came to the Olympic Stadium and saw this event. They saw that it was well run and ordered. They had feared that a large event run by Pentecostals would be conducted in a disorderly manner without respect for organisation – simply 'as the Spirit led'. They discovered otherwise and, too late, became quite enthusiastic about it.

'There was immense blessing for all those who attended. We saw three things that weekend: the tremendous testimony of Christians to Berlin; thousands of people going forward to give their lives to Christ and the first step towards a reconciliation between the Pentecostals and the Evangelical Alliance. Volkhard Spitzer's vision had been for the Berlin Stadium to be filled with people, a Christian witness that would shine like a beacon not only to the Christians in West Germany which no doubt it was, but to those behind the iron curtain as well.

'I have kept in touch with the situation since but I have to say that sadly, as far as I know, there has not been a serious continuation of that reconciliation process. No doubt barriers were broken down but I don't think that enough effort has been made since to continue the process.

'The state of German Christianity behind the iron curtain is a different matter. There is a lot said about how little freedom there is but it is not as bad as it is sometimes made out to be. There are "three levels" of persecution in Eastern Europe. First of all the State does keep an eye on the institutionalised church, that is those churches that are registered by the State. The government registers them and monitors them but generally they don't interfere.

'The second level of persecution is more personal. If you have declared that you are a Christian then it is likely that you and your children will not get the best opportunities and you have to sacrifice some earthly hopes but again physical interference is usually minimal.

'The third level is more severe. That is when the churches and their members get involved at the political level. They use their Christianity as an anti-communist tool. They refuse to register their churches. They often meet in the open air and they openly defy the authorities. If we were to try and hold an evangelistic meeting in the open in this country, certainly in the cities, we would soon find out just how much freedom of speech we have here – the police would soon be along to break up the obstruction.

'The experience I've had of the iron curtain churches has been of a much livelier faith than that in the West. I remember once I was invited to preach in both East and West Berlin on the same Sunday. In the morning I was at a gospel church in East Berlin, we had great fellowship, there was no attempt made to influence my preaching. I preached a gospel-based sermon to about four hundred and fifty people. After the message the pastor invited me back for lunch. The pudding was a special treat – cornflakes! In the evening I was preaching in West Berlin. About thirty-five people attended the service and I was greeted with the usual formal and cold attitudes that so many of the churches in the West reveal. I have long since come to believe that Western Europe is in a post Christian era. We need to bring Christianity back from the Third World and the enthusiasm and fervour that should go with it.'

11: Malta

Malta went to the polls for a general election in
December 1981. It was to be a battle royal between the
then Prime Minister, Dom Mintoff and his Socialist
Party and a newly strengthened democratic opposition,
the Nationalist Party led by Dr Edward Fenech-Adami.
  Harvey has close links with the International Democrat Union (IDU), the organisation that links the Christian Democrats and the Conservative parties of the world
and which supports the parties in their various countries.
Harvey was invited by Eddie Fenech-Adami and his
party to come and share in the elections with the
Nationalist Party.
  'Mintoff (whose daughter threw cow dung down into
the chamber of the House of Commons a few years ago)
was what might be called a Fascist/Communist dictator.
In other words he was a right-wing dictator on the one
hand, but like most dictators the people who are most
friendly to him are the Communist regimes. For example
Mintoff has negotiated agreements with the Soviet
Union so that they can refuel their Mediterranean ships
through Malta's docks. I think it's a pity that Cunard
has sent ships for servicing in Malta, because although
the price is competitive it is being subsidised, albeit
indirectly, by the Soviet Union.
  'We went to Malta in 1981 first to observe and to see
if we could be of help in the election. We met, chatted

and shared some of the experiences we had had of setting up and running campaigns.

'Popular support for Eddie Fenech-Adami's Nationalist Party had become considerable and this had not escaped the notice of Mintoff. Aware that his position was threatened before the 1981 election, he changed certain constitutency boundaries. His gerrymandering was skilfully done.

'In Malta they elect on the basis of Proportional Representation. Each constituency can return five members to Parliament. On this system each candidate must get one sixth of the votes plus one – that would be enough to allow them a certainty of getting in. In most constituencies three people are returned for one party and two from the other, sometimes it goes four to one.

'Mintoff realised that it was likely that he was not going to get his majority if the boundaries remained the same because a swing to the Nationalists would change the proportions. The Nationalist Party got fifty-one per cent. of the votes, but still did not get into government. Fifty-one per cent., should be a majority in any country but Mintoff had moved blocks of labour voters from heavy Labour constituencies into less secure areas to counter the swing and it worked!

'Eddie Fenech-Adami had a super team working for him. They are sophisticated in that they understood the *concepts* of PR and what needed to be done. They could apply those concepts in the most simple terms. I helped with the Election Rallies for Eddie – in the last one we had forty thousand people in the stadium at Valetta.

'Being with them at this time was an interesting, if sometimes a frightening experience. Mintoff had control of the Army, the media, the police and television and he used the lot for his own propaganda. No broadcasting by the Nationalist Party was permitted.

'The Nationalists did get around that for a while. In

England we got hold of the complete equipment for a TV transmitter station. That was shipped to Sicily which is sixty miles away from Malta and for two weeks the people in Malta had a choice of viewing. It took Mintoff a fortnight to find the engineers (who came from Italy) who could jam the broadcasts, so in the last week running up to the election we could not transmit successfully but at least the dictator saw a spark of freedom.

'Not only did Eddie Fenech-Adami have trouble in transmitting his message to his people but we all had difficulty in communicating outside of Malta. My 'phone calls to Marlies (who had been unable to come) were tapped and frequently cut off. I would hear voices and then the dialling tone. Certainly as things hotted up and I tried to get confirmation to her and to the British media, things became almost impossible.

'On the morning that they were to announce the result, guns started going off in Valletta and there was a huge military presence. Helicopters were flying about and armoured jeeps raced round the streets.

'At this point we thought that Mintoff had discovered he'd lost and had swung a military coup, so we tried to get in touch with Britain. I had enough time to call and tell Marlies get in touch with BBC Newsnight and tell them to expect my call. When I did get through, of course Mintoff's police cut me off. Then we managed to get a radio telephone and go up on to the roof. It took them three minutes to trace that, enough time for me to talk to the BBC.

'Malcolm Thornton, who is an MP, and who was the official observer for the Conservative Party also tried to get information back to his local radio news programme and to Independent Radio News (IRN). Mintoff had banned the London *Times* and the BBC from Malta so we had to make a covert arrangement with the BBC. I did an interview with Eddie on a high band U-matic video tape. I asked the questions for the BBC and filmed Eddie answering them. We had arranged with the BBC that someone would fly in from London to pick up the tape. A girl arrived, she had flown in as a tourist on an ordinary flight. She collected the tape, got in a taxi, went straight back to the airport and caught the last flight back to London before snow shut down the airports in Britain. It went on TV that evening.

'The actual counting of the votes took about three days and as we were meant to be observers, several of us thought we'd like to go and observe the counting. We were myself and Malcolm Thornton, Roger Boaden from Conservative Central Office, a few others and Otto Von Hapsburg, who for a few hours as a three-month-old baby had been the last Emperor of the Austro-Hungarian Empire. (There is a story, probably apocryphal, that says that when he was in the European Parliament recently, someone said to him "Austria and Hungary are playing tonight", to which he is reputed to have said "Oh really, who are we playing?"! He is also the person cited by the weird book "The Holy Blood and the Holy Grail" as the blood descendant of Christ.)

'We approached, by car, the military barracks where the counting was taking place. When we got to the military checkpoint, we were stopped by soldiers with machine guns and asked our business. When we said we wanted to go in and observe the proceedings and the count we were told that we couldn't. Any member of the Press could (which I was) but I would have to walk the three miles to the barracks and stay there for the full three days of the count. Since we already had observers in there and the Press was there too we decided it wasn't worth the bother. We asked the lieutenant how the count was going:

' "Oh everything is going fine" he replied, "And Mr Mintoff will win again".

'We went back and waited. The television blared out the Mintoff propaganda. "Socialist victory! Socialist victory!" it said. They ran the film "The Railway Children" about seven times and then as it became clearer that Mintoff's gerrymandering might keep him in with a Parliamentary majority, they began to play a tape of Leslie Crowther and others singing the song "Run Rabbit Run". Eddie's middle name "Fenech" is Maltese for "rabbit". More nastily, on the morning of the result, Mintoff supporters went round and put dead rabbits with their throats cut on the steps of the meetings places of the Nationalist Party supporters.

'It was impossible however, to hide the support that Eddie had. Out of a population of three hundred thousand, he managed to get a crowd of forty thousand to a rally in a football stadium in Valletta.

'Mintoff himself, has now retired, probably because he knows that no amount of fiddling the boundaries will keep him in power in the 1986 elections. His Deputy Prime Minister, Mr Bonici has taken over the socialists. Bonici was the fellow who, in the Autumn of 1984, ordered the Socialist supporters to help the army keep the Roman Catholic schools shut to try to make the Catholics offer free education. He also led the mob who wrecked the Archbishop's curia that same year. It is a tragedy that the thousands of people of Malta have had to suffer through such disgraceful leaders.

'Before the election, I helped with a few rallies. One of them turned out to be a bit tense. We had forty thousand people in the Valletta stadium and Eddie was to be the main speaker but he was addressing another meeting on the neighbouring island of Gozo. The rally was to last three or four hours and started with one-and-a-half-hours of entertainment, mainly rock groups. It was a development of what we have done in rallies with Mrs Thatcher, starting by entertaining and then focussing in on the political point. We had rock musicians from Italy, (it's amazing how many of them are English, well known in Italy but not heard of here). We used two adjacent stages, one for the entertainment and one for the politicians. I was by the stage producing and I was in walkie-talkie contact with the people at the gates. The rally was progressing nicely but as it went on there was still no sign of of Eddie arriving back from Gozo. We had two Italian ex-Prime Ministers (there are plenty of Italian ex-Prime Ministers) so I put one up on the stage to do his speech. He spoke for ten or fifteen minutes and as he was coming to the end of his speech I called round again "Any sign of Eddie?".

' "No, no sign yet." came the reply.

'So we put the second Italian Prime Minister on the stage and he did his ten minute address. I called round again "Any sign of Eddie?"

' "Still no sign, he's on the boat from Gozo, it's been delayed." The boat from Gozo took about half an hour and then it was another ten minutes from the docks to the stadium. By then we were running out of people to put on stage, so I persuaded the Nationalist Party's International Secretary to make a speech. A bit stuck for a subject, he went up and said in Maltese "The speech the last speaker made in Italian was so good that I'm going to repeat it in Maltese" and he did!

'By this time we had heard that Eddie had arrived at the gate but the crowds were so thick that the driver couldn't see where he was going and he made slow progress towards us but we did finally get him on stage.

'The rally was fantastic and the election campaign brought in fifty one per cent. of the votes. Eddie may not have won enough seats in that election but his chances are much greater in the next one.

'Mintoff was not unaware of our presence. It seems that he was so worried by our help to the Nationalists that soon after the election he passed a law called the "Foreign Interference Bill". This Bill said that no foreigner could give any assistance to any Maltese party and no Maltese living abroad is allowed to visit or take part in any political event, nor is any foreigner. That, of course, only applies to the Nationalists because Mintoff brought in and still does bring in a great deal of foreign help.

'The International Democrat Union is an organisation through which initiative has been taken by the leaders of the conservative parties, with the assistance of Scott Hamilton who has really pulled the organisation together.

'The conservative parties of the world have, for a long time, been reacting to a situation rather than taking the initiative. The socialists have long since had an international movement that finds and gives moral support to the "socialist struggle" in various countries.'

In July 1985, in Washington there was a meeting of IDU Party Leaders. There were seven heads of government. The meeting lasted a day and a half and as Harvey points out was, in many ways bigger than a Summit meeting. Speaking before the meeting, Harvey was anticipating some familiar presentation difficulties.

'Two heads of state will be speaking at a banquet on the evening of the meeting. They will speak one after the other and the range in their "eye level" height is from five foot two to six foot three (Mrs Thatcher to George Bush).'

Once again the problem for Harvey was the lectern, although this one was electronic it was not moveable by remote control.

'The one I designed for the Conservative Conferences back home could be adjusted from a distance, but the American one at this conference you had to alter by flicking a switch on the thing itself.

'It's very hard to be unobtrusive when you're six foot four and eighteen stone but someone will have to go up on to the stage and change the height and they will only have one minute to do it. I still don't know whether that person will be me or whether I'll arrange for someone more attractive to do it!'

While the Americans have taught Harvey the techniques of smooth presentation the different demands of varying political situations means that the implementation of those techniques and its technology also varies.

'In many ways the Americans are not as sophisticated as we are, they are certainly much more specialised than we are. Over here we have to present various public faces, cabinet ministers, party spokesman, and the Prime Minister. In America they have a big team working exclusively for the President. They only have to present the President, so they don't have to worry too much about differing heights of lecterns or the presentation of different faces.'

Harvey's role in the July meeting was as security liaison with the Americans (no small task with the expected arrival of seven heads of state) and more familiarly, co-ordination with the media.

Harvey does not usually attend banquets, although as a member of the team he is always welcome.

'Just occasionally I'll stick myself on an outer table where I can get up and walk about without anyone noticing. As with all these things I can't really take part in the occasion and stage manage it as well. I will put on a dinner jacket in order not to stand out but if you want to be sure that things are running properly you can't be sitting at a table delicately handling your fish.

'It's hard to be a back room boy and a front room boy, although I've had to do it quite a bit. All the time you're speaking you're thinking "Is the mike at the right level?" "Are the fold-back speakers in the right place?"

If you're thinking all that while you're performing you can't really concentrate on producing the show. I recall one evening meeting when I had not only to plan, organise and run the thing but to compere it as well.

'It was ridiculous, half an hour before I was due to go on stage I was on my hands and knees, sticking down wires with gaffer tape. I had no real time to prepare my questions or my links in the running order, nor did I have time to get washed or cleaned up. I just had to slap on some deodorant, put a jacket and tie on, and get on stage.

'It is possible to both run and participate in an event but it is safer, if not less stressful, to remain behind the scenes. As a backstage man it's my job to make sure that other people come over well, to make sure that everything is clear, that their voices can be heard, so that when they make a mistake it comes over clear as a bell!'

Despite his protestations that he likes being and should remain a backstage man, his early training in radio and in television have left him with one hankering for a specific kind of high profile role in front of the microphone.

'I would really like to present a gospel pop show in this country. I used to present one on KAIM in Hawaii and if the opportunity arose here I would jump at it!'

Briefly but crucially, at the Brighton Conference, Harvey was to find himself in front of the microphone. Then the lights, the sound and the technical presentation were all taken care of by somebody else, all he had to do was communicate as effectively as he could.

12: Rescued

'Harvey we can't get this stuff off your chest.' Without
lifting gear the rescue was proving arduous. I called
back "Could you jack it up and get the weight off my
chest then you could pull me out?" And that's how we
did it. They got a hydraulic jack and began to lift the
weight off me, which was a great relief – at last I could
take a proper breath.

"Tell us when you think we can get you out" said
Ken and when I did, I forced my hands back and
grabbed hold of one of the firemen. Two more firemen
grabbed hold of him, they pulled and I kicked and
struggled through this short tunnel they had made. I
came out like a pea from a pod, minus a few layers of
skin but otherwise unhurt.'

It was Ken Towner who had reached down and
grabbed hold of Harvey. 'I put my arms under his back
and across his chest and I tried to pull for all I was
worth. He came out like a rabbit and the people behind
me just grabbed him and pulled him out further leaving
me floundering knee deep in the rubble!'

'I did however, have two quarter-inch stones
embedded in my right ear by the blast. These came out
a fortnight later. I flew to Montreal, via New York and
when I landed the pressure seemed to shift something
in my ear and one quarter inch stone fell out. Then
when I flew up to Montreal, again the pressure seemed

to do something to the middle ear and the other stone dropped out. I was still left with some grit embedded in the ear and that was not cleared until February, four months later.

'I had also swallowed quite a bit of grit and as I came out I choked on it and spat it out "That's right, cough it up!" I heard a fireman say.

'What I didn't know then but soon realised, was that the rescue had been filmed by ITN with the help of their lights, so as soon as I reached the open air, almost before in fact, the firemen had wrapped a blanket round me. I had gone to bed in only a T-shirt which was now in tatters. The ITN film shows too that one of the firemen said "I'll get you some water to clear the rubble from your eyes" and he went off camera to return only seconds later with a *cup* of fresh water. I took it entirely for granted at the time, I thought that he had got it from the water gushing down from the pipes, but it was clean not filthy as the rubbled water would have been and it was in a cup. I still don't know where he got it from or how, so quickly.'

It seems that the cup and the water came from one of the rooms. Although Harvey's room had been blown away, much of the hotel was still standing, even functioning and so one of the firemen did the obvious thing and went to one of the rooms to get the water. After all, as Ken Towner said 'It was a hotel!'

'The first thing they asked me when I was pulled clear was "Was there anyone else in the room?" I replied that there had been no one else. They hadn't asked me that while I was under the rubble, I assume because if Marlies had been there it could have worried me, especially as there was no sound from anyone else.

'Once they had established that there was no one else buried there I remember asking them where I was. "On the fifth floor" they replied.

101

' "Okay" I said. "I can walk down from here." I assumed that they would be needed somewhere else and that since I could walk I should now look after myself. The firemen had other ideas and insisted on carrying me. (Although I was told later by one of them "If we'd known how big you were we'd have left you there and found someone else to dig out!".) They still could not be sure that I was as unhurt as I looked, or that shock would not take over. They carried me down in a blanket, it took eight of them to do it. We went down the main stairs, although how they got me out of the hotel I can't remember, because at that time Norman Tebbit was still trapped over the main door. As we went down I asked about Mrs Thatcher. She was the first person I thought about then because I knew, of course, that Marlies was safe in London. "We can't say much" they replied. "but she has been seen leaving the hotel, apparently all right."

'Once down, they put me in the ambulance and I was taken to the Royal Sussex County Hospital. The ambulance, it appeared, was not a local one because, as I lay there, I could hear this debate going on between the driver and his colleague as to how to get to the hospital.

' "I'm sure it's up this hill" said one.

' "No, I'm sure it's round this next corner."

'It took us slightly longer to reach the hospital because of this confusion and by this time, I was becoming more concerned about Marlies. Although it was still dark I knew that I had been under the rubble for some time. It was important that I tell her soon that I was safe. I knew that she was going to get up early and watch Breakfast Television because the previous day I had recorded interviews with both channels about the preparation for the Prime Minister's Rally.

' "What time is it?" I asked as soon as I got to the hospital.

' "Quarter to six" they replied. They had dug me out at five twenty-five. The bomb exploded at two fifty-four!

'Let me give someone a telephone number. Would somebody ring my wife and tell her that I am all right. She will be getting up early to watch Breakfast TV. She is five days overdue with our first baby and the signs are that it will arrive today.' I asked if I could call her myself and they replied that I could, after a check-up. A man went off with the telephone number and called Marlies. Not only that, he came back and told me that he had done so.

' "I've told her there's been a slight accident but that you're all right and that you will speak to her yourself soon." It was a great relief to know that Marlies knew that I was OK.

'She actually was not at all surprised to hear that I had had a slight accident so early in the morning. She thought I had fallen off a ladder because at that particular conference we had had a recurring problem with the slogan "Britain Winning Through". The "G" in "Winning" kept falling off and I had often had to climb up a ladder to stick this large polystyrene letter back on the wall.

'I was examined by the medical staff and it was soon established that there was no structural damage. They had to cut the T shirt off me. The doctor told me that he thought I was all right but that I would probably suffer from shock.

'Once I had realised that I was fundamentally all right I asked them if I could discharge myself. They told me that I could but that they would not advise it and suggested that I stay in for a while. "Not likely" I said "that's my conference going on out there." I was in no doubt that since Mrs Thatcher was all right she would decide that the conference would go on as usual but secretly I was a bit worried about what they might do to it if I wasn't there! This is a perfectly normal paranoia for a Conference Organiser!'

Organising conferences was so much second nature to Harvey now that even in such a crisis it was his first thought. It involves administration, co-ordination, timing and experience, and while the bomb had done physical damage to the people and the place, it might also damage the image and presentation of the conference. It was important that the message communicated to the terrorists and to the world, was that the normal running of democracy could not be intimidated or threatened by violence. That destruction could not swerve the course of democratic decision making, that the ballot box was more powerful than any bomb.

13: Response and Reflection

The process of organising a conference begins before anyone invited has put the dates down in their diary. The principles of such organisation Harvey learned many years before with the Billy Graham Team. His private office is full of evidence of that training and influence. Early in his organising career he was told by Bill Brown, now President of World Wide Pictures the Billy Graham film Organisation, to compile 'Procedure Books'. These books, or large A4 lever arch files, line the walls of his office. A copy of everything relevant to a certain conference or rally has been taken, holes punched in it, or it is mounted on a piece of paper into which the holes are punched. These holes are reinforced and the relevant piece of information placed in the file. There are flow charts, conference running orders, photographs, press cuttings. Letters to people inviting them to speak, duplicated circulars, stickers and bills. These records have become a basis from which Harvey can work on any project. They provide the principles of organisation as well as the memories of each event and the people involved. Harvey's techniques are not copyrighted. More than once he has received information from parallel rallies (perhaps a colleague in the Billy Graham Team also setting up a crusade) and sat reading the information conscious of a feeling of 'déjà vu', only to realise that what he is reading, although changed in the details, is his own wording and style. He finds it encouraging that the principles he has implemented have become established in the Christian world and are becoming more recognised in commercial and political awareness.

He can also claim to have 'discovered' a young woman by the name of Stephanie Wills, a girl who started as his secretary and assistant and through hard work and dedication was soon spotted and employed by Billy Graham himself. She is now his personal secretary.

The object of a conference, religious or political, is to provide a forum for debate for the participants and a way of getting the message across to the public who observe. Certainly the Conservative Party's annual conference (as with all the political conferences) is a show piece for the Party, as are some of the foreign tours that the more senior politicians undertake.

Any failure in the presentation of a speech or conference can be embarrassing not only for the individual but for the Party and its image.

'There are two objects of the exercise: to make things easy for the speakers to deliver and to make it easy for the audience to receive the communication.'

All this, Harvey claims, must be done without too much awareness by those two sections of a conference. The preparation has to be done properly and far enough in advance. Years of experience have enabled Harvey to achieve these objects, but experience is not only the result of correct decision making but also the ability to learn from mistakes.

The Newcastle conference, the first Conservative conference held after the Brighton bombing was untouched by terrorism, but a breakdown in communications did provide Harvey with work to do.

'It was Saturday lunch time in Newcastle and the Prime Minister had arrived and was going on the stage

– actually walking on to the stage. I was standing at the foot of the stairs making sure that everyone was getting up there safely and the Chairman of the meeting said to me, as he was walking on to the stage himself, "Harvey, I think we will have the National Anthem at the end of this speech, after all."

'I had one of those awful heart stopping moments, because, as usual, no one had actually given me a detailed programme and everyone had said that they would rather have "The Blaydon Races" at the end – well it *was* Newcastle! I had carefully lined up the music for the Blaydon Races on the tape machine. We don't always have the National Anthem and a decision, I thought, had been made to have "The Blaydon Races". "Well, we would like to have the National Anthem after all" I was told.

'I walked round the front and made sure that everything got started smoothly, that the autocue was right, that the lectern worked, the lights were all right and the microphones on. Mrs Thatcher started her speech and I listened to about thirty seconds. Then I shot out of the back and got two policemen in a police car to take me out of the conference. The barriers were solid at one hundred yards and no one could get through quickly. So the policemen gave me a ride out through them and down into a pedestrian precinct, along which we cruised slowly. We stopped by a record shop and I dashed in saying "I need a cassette of the National Anthem."

'They looked everywhere under "N" for National, "A" for Anthem "E" for Elgar (because he wrote it) and they couldn't find anything. And Mrs Thatcher's speech was progressing fast! At last they found a recording of the last night of the Proms. It started off with a bit of waffle from the conductor but otherwise it was OK. Well of course, I didn't have a record player so I borrowed the record and charged out of the shop and down the street to a Lasky's shop, followed at a sedate pace by the Police car. We persuaded the Lasky's manager to dub the Anthem on to cassette. I went with the newly taped National Anthem on a cassette back through the barriers into the Conference and over to the sound man. As I ran I lined up the tape so that we did not hear the conductor's waffle. I handed it to the sound man who cued it up just as Mrs Thatcher sat down at the end of her speech!'

Mrs Thatcher's trip to Washington to give her celebrated speech to the American Congress also presented some logistical problems. In one sense Harvey was on home ground. He is no stranger to the techniques and approaches of his American counterparts but in other ways they were on foreign soil. In particular Harvey could not take with him the hydraulic lectern that he fought so hard to introduce in Britain. Congress has an immovable lectern and it was too high for Mrs Thatcher.

'We had one day in which to build a platform, four feet wide, six inches high and twelve feet long. The professionalism of my American colleagues is to be envied. Not only did they build the platform but they carpeted it too, in the same colour as Congress's carpet, so that no one need know that anything special had been done.

'In Washington I noticed several differences between their methods and ours. They are altogether less cumbersome! The whole thing was recorded by remote controlled cameras and the TV lighting was both better and more economic. They only light the areas that need lighting. They do not blind the participants with an array of powerful film and camera lights on the basis of the British TV approach which is "If it's within half a mile – floodlight it!"

'They approached the problem of lighting with subtlety and sophistication. We decided what we wanted lit and gave it two hundred foot candles worth with very little spill over. The BBC use the most light of all. They always have much more lighting than any other TV company. This is not helpful to us, particularly when setting up the autocue. Arranging light for the autocue is always a headache in Britain. The screens, off which the speaker reads, are glass and if the light is not angled properly it can act as a reflector or suffer from glare. It is a delicate job and you have to set the lights not only to prevent glare but so that you don't dazzle your speaker either. It is even more tricky when we use large screen TV as well.

'Working closely with trusted professional colleagues such as Ken Oxley at BBC TV News and Doug Wilkins and Pete Hubberd at ITN has been a real pleasure for years. Relations with the Press and the media are, of course, a major part of setting up a conference or rally. Microphones and sound have to be right. Interviews and Press Conferences have to be arranged.

'Organising and liaising with the media must also happen in the wake of a major announcement or a disaster. Whenever there is a catastrophe, like the one in Brighton, the Press are desperate to know, to get the story and to pass the message on to the public. In Brighton though, for a long time, it was difficult for the Press to find out what had happened and what was going to happen.

Harvey, in the meantime, was speaking to Marlies.

' "There's been a bomb" (I don't know when I realised that it had been a bomb, or whether anyone had told me but I knew by now what had happened. "I'm absolutely fine," I went on. "but my room and everything in it has disintegrated, I've got no clothes, nothing. Can you get some clothes together and catch the first train down to Brighton. I'm at the Royal Sussex

County Hospital." So Marlies and my mother, who was staying with her while she was waiting for the birth, gathered together what I needed and started to make their way to Brighton. I had forgotten to mention to Marlies that I needed shoes too but in all the rush she still remembered and brought my only other pair with her.

'The next 'phone call I made at about five fifty-five was to Maria Thompson, my secretary who was staying in another hotel. "Hello" I said, when she answered sleepily. "I'm in the hospital."

' "Great!" she exclaimed. "How's Marlies?" She, of course, thought that I had dashed back to London in response to a call from Marlies to say that she was in labour. I explained what the real situation was and said "Look, get down to the conference hall and do everything that we would normally do in preparation. Make sure that everything is ready to go."

'Once that call was made, there was little more I could do except wait, or so I thought, but the demands of the press were becoming more insistent. While I was waiting for the plastic skin on my legs to settle so that I could wash, one of the Hospital Administrators came down and said to me "We need someone who can give some interviews to the press and answer questions. Would you do it? You're the only one not in shock!" Most of the others were seriously hurt and suffering. Besides, dealing with the press was also my job. "We'd be grateful," said the Administrator "It will mean that the media will stop bugging us. They keep wanting to get into bedrooms to get answers to their questions."

'I said that that would be fine, so they put me in a wheelchair (I was still wrapped in the blanket and filthy, I couldn't borrow any clothes, because I was too big, I still have to get most of my clothes in America). So clothed only in a blanket I went to meet the Press. The

110

room was full of lights, so I couldn't see anything beyond them because of the dazzle.

'It turned out to be a sizeable press conference but at the time I didn't know that. I did interviews for the BBC and American television. The American interview was flashed across the States at Breakfast time, so in the afternoon many of my friends were ringing to find out how I was. The BBC interview was repeated throughout the morning.

'When I did those interviews, I told it just as it happened. I spoke of my faith which had given me spiritual strength under the tons of rubble. I talked of my prayer that I would see my darling Marlies again and our little baby. I told them too that I thought the Conference should and would go ahead. I had no right to make that decision but I knew very well what Mrs Thatcher would say. Once the interviews were finished, I was able to get cleaned up.

'While I waited for Marlies and my mother to arrive I had six baths and washed my hair four times. The hospital had covered me in plastic skin to help my abrasions and grazes heal but that stiffened me up. After the first two baths the nurse had to come and scrape out the dust and debris that gathered in the bottom of the bath. It was too much to go down the plughole!

Marlies arrived about nine o'clock, and although I was cleaned up and okay, I think the sight of me wrapped in a blanket and sitting in a wheelchair gave her a bit of shock. But I soon got dressed and we went together down to the Conference Hall. I was ten minutes late, the only time I've ever been late for a Conference and *that* was due to British Rail's slow, slow train to Brighton that arrived late as always.

'When I got into the Conference Hall I was warmly welcomed by many of my friends. It seemed that I was actually an encouragement to them, for one minute they

111

had seen me on the television, in a wheelchair, describing my time under the rubble and the next minute there I was, in the Conference Hall and ready to go. I did not realise at the time how much TV time I had occupied.'

Harvey's presence did not go unnoticed. 'Then, bless his golden heart, Harvey Thomas came into the room. He had been trapped under the rubble but there he was and I was just so thankful that someone who been through all those last terrible hours could still be so remarkably cheerful and keep going.' Mrs Thatcher later told Douglas Keay of "Woman's Own" when she described her own experience of the bombing.

'We decided' Harvey says 'not to put her speech on autocue. It is a very useful tool in helping you to communicate with an audience but we felt that on this occasion it was not appropriate.'

'Working for Mrs Thatcher, in many ways, is very little different from working with Billy Graham. They are both genuine people with total conviction about the rightness of what they are doing. They are not doing it for the money or to be famous, but because they are convinced in their hearts that it is what they *should* be doing.

'Both are people of enormous vision and by that I don't mean "vision" in the "picture" sense of the word, I mean long-term vision. Billy Graham wants to preach the gospel to the whole world, Mrs Thatcher wants Britain back on top of the world in terms of people, achievement and national pride.

'They are both quite unashamed of what they're doing because it's *right*, so they do it without inhibition. They will both listen to criticism but if they are convinced of the rightness of the course, they will continue in the face of opposition. Both Billy Graham and Margaret Thatcher can delegate but if they ever do get involved in the details, they *really* get involved!

'One of the hazards of being such a person, a leader of a party or of a team and of working with them, is that their word can be taken as law even when it is not intended that way. I remember once with Billy Graham we had been given some mineral water and Billy liked it very much. He commented on it and said "Hey, we should have this at all our crusades." Not long after that I was in Australia and these two crates of mineral water arrived. I enquired as to where they were coming from and discovered that someone had taken Billy at his words and crates of the stuff were being bought for every crusade.

'Mrs Thatcher also enjoys mineral water – as long as it is British. I have Ashbourne Water for her and I even took a crate to Washington DC for the address to Congress. The officials didn't want to allow me to put a bottle by the lectern. "It's commercial" they said.

' "No it isn't" I said. "It's British!" and I won!

'Both Billy Graham and Mrs Thatcher are excellent communicators, Mrs Thatcher is perhaps slightly more reserved than Billy but then Billy is an orator. His prime task and talent is oratory and he uses it for one basic message. Mrs Thatcher's prime task is government and its complexities. But Mrs Thatcher is also an excellent "huge crowd" speaker and I wish we had more opportunity for her – perhaps using satellites as Billy did from Sheffield in July 1985.

'Working for the two different people has its similarities but the causes are different, Brian Shallcross of Television South spotted that when I first took on the consulting work for the Conservatives. He interviewed me live on what was then Southern Television and asked: "Do you really feel that you can put forward the Conservative message in the same way as you put forward the gospel message?" I said:

"Spiritually, I'm a Christian; politically, I know that

I'm a Conservative and I can put the same enthusiasm into it in the context of the political world"

'He said "Alleluia!" and I rejoined

' "Amen!"

'It would be wrong to say though, that there is no difference between the gospel and politics. Just before the Brighton Conference I was on Newsnight and they asked me. "If you had to choose, which is the more important, the gospel or the political message?" I had to reply that the gospel was more important because the gospel deals with eternal truths and everlasting life – the ultimate questions and answers. The political only deals with life in the short term, in as much as it can only deal with the time we are here on earth and can physically take part in it.'

Mrs Thatcher's speech on the afternoon of the conference after the bomb, met the occasion with the combination of sorrow and resolve that she felt. The Conference in subdued but strengthened mood began to pack up and go home. The elation of the previous night's parties followed by the horror of the bombing, combined to make the last tidying up and packing away a painful chore for Harvey and his colleagues, who now just wanted to get home.

'By the time it came to packing up, even clearing the stage after Mrs Thatcher's speech, I had stiffened up considerably and I was limping quite a bit but apart from that I was fine. Even so I had called the RAC out to change a flat tyre on my car that morning, I really didn't feel up to that. We loaded the usual stuff on to its transport and made sure that everything was on its way and then Marlies, my mother and I made our way to the Royal Albion Hotel, which is where we had booked in.

'I went to have a look at the hole the bomb had made and noticed one of my white T-shirts hanging in tatters, on a bit of rubble where my room had been. Out of room 729 came only three things in one piece: my hardback Bible which I had been given as a twenty-first birthday present. It was battered but complete. My Seiko watch which was found on the third floor still ticking and of course, me.

'We went back to the hotel and switched the TV on for News at Ten. I don't think that even then we fully realised the enormity of the thing that had happened. Until then it was still a personal thing, something that had happened to me, with repercussions on my family. We hadn't really thought of it as a massive terrorist attack, an attempt on the Prime Minister's life that had international significance.

'But then we watched News at Ten and saw what other people had seen – including my own rescue. The newsreader said "The firemen have heard a voice calling under the rubble."

' "There's someone alive in there!"

'And then they started to dig and I saw them working, three of them. The newsreader went on "They have cut a beam to ease the pressure on the man's chest. They know who it is, it's Harvey Thomas, one of the Conference Organisers."

'This was the first time that Marlies had seen what I had gone through and it was quite a shock for her. It was the first time that she realised the magnitude of what had happened to me and how fortunate I had been to survive.

'We did not rest long, all we wanted to do now was to get back home. We packed up and got in the car. We had got no further than Preston Fire station, where all the firemen came from to do the rescue, when the car broke down!'

14: Requiem

Compassion is an aspect of politics and politicians that is not always obvious to the public. It is in the nature of governments and their members that they are sometimes faced with unpopular decisions. Harvey remembers the night when the ship the "Sheffield" was sunk, the first British victim of the Falklands War.

'That night, the night of the sinking, Mrs Thatcher was speaking in Finchley, and those of us who are in her constituency saw a side of the Prime Minister that the public very rarely sees. They do not see the tremendous pain and hurt she can feel as she did that night. They did not see the tears in her eyes at the thought that she was the first British Prime Minister to send her people to war for decades. I wish that more people could see that side of her.

'The public should witness the compassion that we feel. It is not always clear to them that we do care but I hope it will become more so as time goes by.'

It is often only in tragedy that people become sufficiently unashamed of their feelings to express them and show that they care. Mrs Thatcher is not unaware of the pain that the loss of friends and colleagues can bring. Through the efforts of terrorism she has lost a good many of those close to her, not least Airey Neave, killed some years before the Brighton bomb.

Less than a year before the Brighton bombing millions

of people witnessed the murder on television of WPC Yvonne Fletcher. She was a victim of the kind of international terrorism and conflict that the Police and rescue services can so easily become. Her death prompted, the film maker Michael Winner to write to the Daily Mail and suggest that a fund or charity should be set up to place memorials on the spots in Britain where members of the Police force have given their lives in the course of their duties. The response to the letter was immediate and Michael Winner was flooded with donations for what had very quickly become 'his' fund. Having thus been given the responsibility for setting up 'The Police Memorial Fund' Michael Winner rose to the occasion and got the charity going. Its first and most visible result was the service that commemorated Yvonne's death and saw the memorial to her, unveiled by Mrs Thatcher.

Michael Winner asked Harvey to help with the organisation of this service.

'There was a tremendous amount to be done. The coordination of security: dogs, Special Branch, the security was very tight. The whole square had to be shut off to the public. We built six inch high speaking stands and the stand for the Prime Minister and the other Party Leaders. The principles of setting up the service were much the same as any other event, although we had to make sure that the unveiling of the memorial would go smoothly. There was a little rope for Mrs Thatcher to pull to draw back the curtain and I think Michael was convinced that wasn't going to work right up to the time that it did work!

'As usual we had to check that the television cameras could get a good view and that everyone could hear. On that score, I discovered that Police Bands don't play on cue, they have to be counted in. So whereas normally when there is music the bands respond to one visual cue from me, the more formal bands have a different approach. As a consequence there were occasional gaps in the proceedings while we waited for the conductor to count everybody in.

'There was some controversy about the timing of that service, because it seemed to threaten the chances of the hostages in Libya being returned home. It wasn't the time that the service was held that was wrong but the timing of the Libyans pronouncements on the subject. Michael had planned the service months before, how else would we be able to get all the leaders of the major political parties in one place at one time?

'Also there are times when an action may not be politically clever but it is right. Mrs Thatcher subscribes to that view and the ceremony went ahead – to honour Yvonne Fletcher's sacrifice and those of her colleagues was the right thing to do at that time.

'The Yvonne Fletcher Memorial is now a tourist stop on the agendas of London sight-seeing tours. At Michael Winner's suggestion they have taken the parking space away from the front of the Memorial and have built the pavement out so that you can't stop in front of it. I did enjoy watching them take the parking meters away to do that!'

There was one light-hearted moment that Harvey recalls from that rather sad day. He had thought that after his moments in front of the cameras in the aftermath of the Brighton bombing he would be forgotten, but in the reception, after the service, one woman who recalled his predicament, asked him whether he was fully recovered from his injuries. Harvey replied that he was. This conversation took place within the earshot of the Leader of the Opposition, Neil Kinnock who responded quickly to the lady's question with "Hurt? This boy bounced, he was back in the Conference Hall by nine o'clock!"

Harvey was surprised that Neil Kinnock was aware

of his existence and said to him "Oh, I didn't think you knew who I was." to which Neil Kinnock replied "Oh I know who you are and what you're doing!"

While Harvey's injuries in the bombing were minor there were others who suffered great pain and loss. It was in recognition of those losses, but also of the part played by people such as Mick Ayling, Ken Towner and their fellows in the rescue services, in making those losses minimal, that a Charity Concert was planned by John Gummer and Andrew Lloyd Webber to raise money for the charities in Brighton, as a token of thanks.

The performance was the British Premiere of Andrew Lloyd Webber's 'Requiem', a piece inspired itself by the agonies of war and terrorism, its title and subject matter seemed a fitting postscript to the most horrifying assassination attempt in this country's modern history.

The idea came about over a dinner party which both Andrew Lloyd Webber and John Selwyn Gummer attended. Between them it was agreed that it would be appropriate if the British Premiere could have a charitable purpose and that purpose would be to raise money for Brighton. The whole thing was set up in a very short period of time, little more than six weeks by Sir Ian McLeod, Sir Peter Lowe, Robin Nelder and Harvey. At that notice, Placido Domingo, Sarah Brightman and Miles Kingston (the boy soprano) all had to be free and so did the venue, Westminster Abbey. Tickets were sold at forty pounds, twenty-five pounds and five pounds. The five pound tickets were for seats where you could hear but not see the performers. The response was immense and fifteen hundred people had to be turned away.

Besides being a very swiftly organised event it was a time for childhood memories to come back for Harvey's connections with the Abbey go back to his old school days. As Harvey was setting up in the Abbey he recalled that the only time he had ever been beaten at school was for running through the Abbey cloisters.

'There was always a morning service held in the Abbey and one morning I was late for it and so I ran through the cloisters and got caught. I was beaten by the then captain of the school, I was given six of the best but they managed to break three six foot bamboo canes on me, I was a big fellow even then. I don't suppose it did me much harm, but I can't say that it did me much good either except that I never ran through the Abbey cloisters again.'

Despite problems with overbooking of seats, and the speed at which everything had to be set up, the evening of the Requiem went smoothly and it raised just over twenty-five thousand pounds for the Brighton charities. It was an evening on which to recall the loss and sadness of the night of October 12th, 1984. It was an evening on which to share not only the grief of the individuals of the atrocity, but to recall the wars and the terror that reigns all over the world. 'Requiem' was inspired by the dilemma of a child forced to watch the torture of his own sister or to kill her. What happened at Brighton was another expression of the same violent aggression that dominates so many causes.

Although less than a year afterwards, for the general public, the 'Requiem' was a kind of conclusion to the events of that night in October. For others it still goes on. For some there is permanent loss and permanent injury and for others, like Harvey, there is the memory if not the fear.

In his early travels, Harvey had come to know the meaning of faith and to rest in the Lord for his ultimate fate. He had lost his fear of flying, he had been inspired to take up the path and career that led him to the Grand Hotel but he had also been prepared by his faith to overcome the fear.

120

15: A New Arrival

For those who had been hurt in the Grand Hotel or who had known someone who was, the following days and months were to be a time of grief and a hard fight to recovery. For a few, there would be no recovery and for others there would be permanent scars. For Harvey and Marlies there was relief and the opportunity, so nearly lost, to look forward together to the birth of their daughter.

'There is a time to be solemn and serious but I sometimes think that it is a little put on. You find yourself a part of some terrible event or witnessing it. No one has to *tell* you to be serious or solemn when you know the full horror of the thing.

'At the same time, if you have survived, if you have got something to look forward to, if like me, some of the things that happened to you are mildly amusing, then I think it's false to hide that.

'In that sort of situation, without being offensive or uncaring, you should do and say what comes naturally. When I was being flung in the air by the explosion I really did think "Is it an earthquake? No it can't be not at a Tory Party Conference" I didn't think "Oh dear something terrible is happening, I must be serious" The situation was perfectly obvious and I had to respond to it genuinely which included some humour.'

Death, perhaps more so than injury, is a subject not

easily dealt with in this country. For years it has been taboo, amongst friends at least, despite the fact that it is flung across our television screens with instant regularity. It is not a light matter, especially for those who are left behind but it is nevertheless an inescapable fact which can have a positive and less solemn side.

One of his greatest challenges as a PR man is Harvey's Directorship with the London Cremation Company. That this work might be considered odd is perhaps an indication in itself of the paranoia surrounding the subject but Harvey tries to help deal with it.

'I find the cremation work interesting. Your interest always grows when you get involved in something. When it crosses your path you like to take a deeper interest in it. It is hard though, to communicate a service to people which depends upon death. You can't go to somebody in PR terms and say "Come and be cremated with us, how about it?" In America they are a little more open about it. I remember in California in a cemetery near to the famous Forest Lawn, there was an ad. saying "Reserve your plot now with the most beautiful views in California". What interest is the view going to be?

'We are getting Hospices here now, places where people who are terminally ill can go to learn how to die and where relatives learn how to face the death of a loved one. I still find that rather foreign to me, but if it helps people then that's good.

'Death is a very objective event. That was something I learned from the bomb. I didn't really have time to realise that this was happening to me. I had no time to meditate on death. I thought I was going to die so I talked to the Lord and I prayed about Marlies and what was going to be Leah and just waited to get on with it, quite objectively. Perhaps that's what a Hospice tries to do. When it starts happening to you the enormity is so subjective that you have to make it objective!

122

'My role on the Board of the London Cremat[...]
Company is a sensitive one in helping with PR. T[...]
Company owns two private Crematoria, Golders Gree[...]
and one in Woking. Because something is difficult to
deal with, that doesn't mean you don't have to sell the
service. It's a mistake we make in the Church. We say
that because something is very personal we shouldn't
try to persuade people to come in, that's interference in
their personal lives! But they need the gospel, in the
same way as when you have a dead body, however
personal it may be, you need to dispose of it properly.

'I remember the first time I was taken round Golders
Green Crematorium I asked my guide "Tell me, do you
keep the ovens at a constant temperature, or do you
have to change the temperature according to the size of
the body." He looked at me very seriously and replied
firmly "Cremators, Mr Thomas, not ovens, we cremate
people, we do not cook them!" '

The Press were looking for a happy ending to one of
the stories of the Grand Hotel. The fact of the imminent
birth of their child did not escape the notice of the Press.
Harvey found himself on Breakfast Television again, this
time with Marlies. He recounted his experience of the
bomb and Marlies of her reaction and the fact that she
was now eight days overdue and everyone held their
breath with Harvey and Marlies.

The great day came on October 18th, six days after
the bomb. By this time the hospital had become aware
that there was to be a little publicity surrounding the
birth of the new arrival. When Marlies was admitted
with labour pains it became clear that a Caesarian operation would be required. A senior consultant carried out
the operation.

For Marlies after the anxiety of the previous week the
birth was not easy either: the night before she had a
contraction which had faded during the day. Then, at

123

one o'clock in the morning the following night the pains began again and this time they went on until four o'clock the next afternoon. At that point, it became clear that a Caesarian was necessary.

Harvey was allowed to stay to watch the operation (the hospital had good evidence for presuming that he was not the panicking or the fainting kind) and very soon Leah Elisabeth was born weighing a bonny seven pounds thirteen ounces. It is Elisabeth spelt with an 's' because she is, of course, half German and that is the German spelling.

It was not until after Leah's birth, when everyone, herself, Harvey and Leah had time to sleep and in Marlies' case think, that the enormity of the events of the previous week really registered. She was given a private room and while Leah was asleep she had time to think that had things been ever so slightly different she might have had to face this alone without Harvey.

The news of Leah's birth took pride of place in the news media. Her proud father is glad to relate that her picture was carried on the front page of 'The Times' and in what Harvey regards as a typical gesture, Mrs Thatcher wrote to Marlies 'A new baby, a new life, a new beginning, a new chance for mankind itself – that is what our lives are all about . . .'

Other Marshall Pickering Paperbacks

DREADLOCKS

Les Isaacs

Les Isaacs knew what it was to hate. He was brought up to believe in England as the land of milk and honey. However, when his parents came here in 1965, he found as a young boy that the cramped basement flats of Islington and the racial prejudice he encountered at school did not match up to the promise. Being tough and independent he became an adept street fighter and by the age of thirteen was leading West Indian gangs in running street battles with white skinheads. The collapse of one dream led him to explore others and in his teens he identified fully with Rastafarian way of life, with its stylish dreadlocks, heavy ganja smoking and vision of liberation from white political and economic slavery. But the inner peace and freedom he sought was not there. Indeed his life was in turmoil.

After a family row he was on the verge of killing his father when he heard a clear proclamation of the Gospel that transformed his life.

The change was complete and the desire to witness to his former friends, other Rastafarians, and young blacks has led him into full-time evangelism in London's deprived inner city areas.

BRITAIN'S TRUE GREATNESS

Peter Toon

Politicians are urging us to 'put the **great** back into Britain'.
But what is the greatness that Britons should desire and seek
from God?

Peter Toon argues that true greatness lies in moral and
spiritual values based on Christianity as a revealed religion.
He examines aspects of our national life to show its moral
and spiritual disease and then points to the prescriptions for
its cure.

Britain's True Greatness is a profound challenge to
British Christians to work towards halting and reversing the
spiritual decline of our country.

NOW I CALL HIM BROTHER

Alec Smith

Alec Smith, son of Ian Smith the rebel Prime Minister of Rhodesia whose Unilateral Declaration of Independence plunged his country into twelve years of bloody racial war, has written his own story of those years.

The story of his life takes him from early years of rebellion against his role as 'Ian Smith's son' through his youth as a drop-out, hippy and drug peddler into the Rhodesian forces.

A dramatic Christian conversion experience at the height of the civil war transformed his life and led to the passionate conviction to see reconciliation and peace in a deeply divided country.

What follows is a thrilling account of how God can take a dedicated life and help to change the course of history.

If you wish to receive *regular information* about *new books,* please send your name and address to:

London Bible Warehouse
PO Box 123
Basingstoke
Hants RG23 7NL

Name _____

Address _____

_____

_____

_____

I am especially interested in:
- [ ] Biographies
- [ ] Fiction
- [ ] Christian living
- [ ] Issue related books
- [ ] Academic books
- [ ] Bible study aids
- [ ] Children's books
- [ ] Music
- [ ] Other subjects

P.S. If you have ideas for new Christian Books or other products, please write to us too!